"True theology is shaped, refined, and informed by the harsh realities of life. In *Embodied Hope*, Kelly Kapic re-examines Christian theology from the vantage point of the ongoing physical suffering that has invaded his own family. This is theology that touches down in real life. It moves from abstract, theoretical notions of God to truth that is necessary for faith to survive. Against the backdrop of human suffering, *Embodied Hope* invites honest engagement with the God who loves us. This book is a gift for those who are wrestling with hard questions and an important resource for ministry leaders in the church and the academy."

Carolyn Custis James, author of *Half the Church* and *Malestrom*

"I am all too familiar with the topic of this book, having lived as a quadriplegic for nearly fifty years and dealing daily with chronic pain. So I'm always heartened when I stumble upon a rich new resource that really encourages. That describes the remarkable book you hold in your hands. Rather than focus on *why*, Kelly makes much of *how*—how to trust God in this world. Best of all, *Embodied Hope* leads the reader to the foot of the cross, the only place to find true relief and healing. I love this book!"

Joni Eareckson Tada, founder and CEO, Joni and Friends International Disability Center

"A famous Christian once described preaching as 'truth through personality.' By that definition, Kelly Kapic's new book is powerful preaching indeed. Kapic presents a range of biblical expositions, all filtered through his deeply personal wrestling with the ongoing chronic pain of his wife and some of his other friends. Here is sermonic theology to comfort, console, and fortify your faith."

Wesley Hill, assistant professor of biblical studies, Trinity School for Ministry, Ambridge, Pennsylvania

"I know of many books about loss. I know of very few books about physical pain, which is the subject of Kelly Kapic's insightful and challenging book. His wife's experience of pain awakened him to the problem, and his broad study and deep reflection prepared him for the writing. Kapic accomplishes what is most difficult. *Embodied Hope* is personal, to be sure. A book like this one almost has to be. But it is also learned and pastoral. He interacts with great minds, both past and present. He explores relevant, even surprising topics, such as the significance of embodiment. Above all he lifts up Jesus Christ as the one who suffers with us and for us, who conquers death, who stands with us. This fresh book does it all. I learned a great deal while reading this book; I also *felt* a great deal. It is the combination of the two that I found so helpful."

Gerald L. Sittser, professor of theology, Whitworth University, author of *A Grace Disguised* and *A Grace Revealed*

"Elegant and accessible, Kelly Kapic's personal and probing book *Embodied Hope* gives a theological exploration of suffering that stands apart from other books. Instead of giving Christian clichés or therapeutic platitudes, Kapic testifies to the way in which the triune God's light shines in the darkness of physical pain, chronic illness, and loss. With pastoral sensitivity and theological insight, Kapic calls the church to live into her God-given identity, even in difficult seasons. I highly recommend it!"

J. Todd Billings, author of *Rejoicing in Lament*

"Kelly Kapic's *Embodied Hope* is a well-written and tremendously helpful theological meditation on pain and suffering, with many examples of ongoing and long-term conditions, including his wife's chronic pain. It is full of biblical realism, acknowledging struggle, confusion, longing, and lament as human in a compassionate and humane way, centered in Christ and his incarnation, suffering, death, resurrection, ascension, and second coming. It also emphasizes the need for loving and prayerful support from one another in the body of Christ and faithfulness in loving God and others in the midst of such chronic pain and suffering. Highly recommended!"

Siang-Yang Tan, professor of psychology, Fuller Theological Seminary, author of *Counseling and Psychotherapy* and *Managing Chronic Pain*

"Out of Kapic's own encounter with pain has come a book that reflects deeply on the theological challenges it poses. As a theological meditation, it helps sufferers dispel distorted images of God and gently nudges them to engage in consideration of God's full identification with us in the incarnate Christ to find an existential answer to an existential problem. Pastors ministering to people facing the enigma of suffering will find here a resource that is at once theologically robust and pastorally sensitive."

Simon Chan, Trinity Theological College, Singapore

"Here is a rare gift of love to the Christian church—especially for sufferers, their watchers, and all who observe deep pain. Kelly Kapic combines love for Scripture, familiarity with the spiritual masters of the past (Athanasius, Luther, and John Owen, to name but a few), and friendship with contemporary sufferers, together with a gracious sensitivity to the sometimes inscrutable wisdom of God. Kapic's reliable and gently applied theology, married as it is to personal experience, offers exactly what the title suggests: embodied hope."

Sinclair Ferguson, teaching fellow, Ligonier Ministries, author of *Deserted by God?*

EMBODIED HOPE

A THEOLOGICAL MEDITATION
ON PAIN AND SUFFERING

KELLY M. KAPIC

IVP Academic

An imprint of InterVarsity Press
Downers Grove, Illinois

InterVarsity Press
P.O. Box 1400, Downers Grove, IL 60515-1426
ivpress.com
email@ivpress.com

InterVarsity Press® is the book-publishing division of InterVarsity Christian Fellowship/USA®, a movement of
students and faculty active on campus at hundreds of universities, colleges, and schools of nursing in the United
States of America, and a member movement of the International Fellowship of Evangelical Students. For
information about local and regional activities, visit intervarsity.org.

Scripture quotations, unless otherwise noted, are from The Holy Bible, English Standard Version, copyright © 2001
by Crossway Bibles, a division of Good News Publishers. Used by permission. All rights reserved.

While any stories in this book are true, some names and identifying information may have been changed to protect
the privacy of individuals.

A small part of chapter one and much of chapter nine in this volume originally appeared in Kelly M. Kapic, "Faith,
Hope, and Love: A Theological Meditation on Suffering and Sanctification," in Sanctification: Explorations in
Theology and Practice, ed. Kelly M. Kapic (Downers Grove, IL: IVP Academic, 2014), 212-31. Used by permission
of InterVarsity Press.

Cover design: David Fassett
Interior design: Jeanna Wiggins
Images: background: © tomograf/iStockphoto
        female silhouette: © Jonathan Knowles / Getty Images
        flower: © posteriori/iStockphoto
        spotted black paper: © GOLDsquirrel/iStockphoto

ISBN 978-0-8308-5179-9 (print)
ISBN 978-0-8308-9097-2 (digital)

Printed in the United States of America ♾

Library of Congress Cataloging-in-Publication Data
A catalog record for this book is available from the Library of Congress.

P	23	22	21	20	19	18	17	16	15	14	13	12	11	10	9	8	7	6	5	4	3	2	1
Y	36	35	34	33	32	31	30	29	28	27	26	25	24	23	22	21	20	19	18	17			

To

Tabitha Kapic

You embody courage and love

I can't thank God enough for you

Jonathan and Margot Kapic

Your faith, joy, and forgiveness are precious gifts to us

&

To those who have supported us so well, especially

Our families and friends

The Covenant College community

New City Fellowship

Lookout Mountain Presbyterian Church

I am poured out like water,
and all my bones are out of joint;
my heart is like wax;
it is melted within my breast.

PSALM 22:14

CONTENTS

A NECESSARY PRELUDE

She didn't just tell me. I was at home with the kids, and she was at the grocery store. The kids played; I messed about the house, picking things up and preparing for dinner. But then, out of nowhere, I was struck with a deep panic. Something was wrong. Suddenly I felt that Tabitha had been gone a bit too long, and I was overcome with strange fears. We had been seeing doctors and going through exams, but, for whatever reason, in that moment these were not the things that came to mind. I tried calling her phone; no answer. I texted. Nothing. Called again—nothing. My initial fears grew exponentially, and without explanation I told my three-year-old daughter and five-year-old son, "Get in the car, hurry."

We started to rush down Lookout Mountain—I knew I would find her car wrecked and thrown from the road and her life in great jeopardy. As I sped down, I held my breath at every bend waiting to see the ambulances, to hear the sirens, and to smell the smoke. But then, halfway down the mountain I saw her driving up in our other car. She gently waved and pointed back up. A deep relief swept over my body. She was okay. No accident. As soon as I could, I turned our car around and headed home.

After the fear that had gripped me I was surprised and relieved to find her calm. We ate a nice little meal, and then she sent the kids off to play in a different part of the house. Sitting me down, she waited till then to tell me the news. She had received the call, and the doctor confirmed she had cancer. While she had been sitting alone in the parking lot of the grocery store with the doctor's voice in her ear, it had started to lightly rain, as if the gentle tears of God were falling upon her.

She had waited, learning long ago a truth she has often repeated to me—"It is always better to tell someone hard things after they have eaten." Well, she had held it together and cared for the family, but now it was time to face reality. Our lives were forever changed. Cancer had infiltrated our family and stricken my wife. There we sat with no answers, not even much energy for questions, just the first waves of grief at what all this would mean. Something terrible had happened on June 9, 2008. It wasn't a car accident, but it did feel like a massive pile of wreckage was threatening to crush us under its weight.

After cancer was detected, I watched my wife courageously and gracefully go through the diagnosis, the surgeries, and the treatments that followed; she would add that she did it imperfectly. Even as I watched her, I was unprepared for the weight of that watching, for the weight of walking beside a suffering one.

Eventually she was declared cancer free. That does not mean scar free or unchanged, but we were thankful. She returned to more normal patterns, actively centering our family, ably engaging in her role at an international humanitarian organization, even enjoying running and hiking with the kids again. We had gotten through the hard thing, and God had preserved us. So much to be thankful for, even amid the challenges.

But then in May 2010 Tabitha called me from the side of the road. She had just been meeting with some pastors about the possibility of planting churches in Haiti. (This was after the devastating earthquake of January 2010.) With uncertainty in her voice she explained, "I'm not sure I can drive home. I don't know what's happening, but there are shooting pains up my legs when I press the clutch or brake." New fears and no good answers. A brain tumor? Multiple sclerosis? What was happening to her body now?

It took us over six years, but we finally got a diagnosis from Mayo Clinic. Tabitha has connective tissue disease, a condition in her experience characterized by debilitating pain in all four limbs, and in her hands and feet. It has not eased through the years; it is slowly moving further up her limbs and remains a daily, even hourly, presence in her and our lives. Somewhere along the way, she also developed a rare disorder called erythromelalgia, or "man on fire" syndrome. Mayo Clinic confirmed this diagnosis as well and the doctor visits and treatment trials continue.

Most people who see her would not guess that this most active and able woman has at times been bedridden or at least severely restricted by her pain and ever-present fatigue. She doesn't like to draw attention to it, which we wrestled through as we debated if we should do this book. Her pain has meant significant changes to all areas of life, from family to church, from work to leisure. If people ask her what has been harder, cancer or dealing with chronic pain, she would certainly say that, in her case, it is the chronic pain. Night or day, there is no getting away from it, like an unwelcome companion who simply will not leave. Always there, always nagging. Always!

Professionally, I am trained as a theologian. I work at a liberal arts college beautifully tucked away on Lookout Mountain, Georgia, overlooking Chattanooga, Tennessee. Although I have a PhD, I find that I rarely know what I think—really think—about something until I have had to write about it. Only as I meditate on Scripture, listen to others, read the reflections of those from centuries past, raise questions, grapple with implications of what I believe, and anticipate objections—not only from others but from my own heart—only then, as I start to put words on the page, do I begin to gain a sense for what I think, even how I feel about something. This may sound strange to others, but it is commonly my experience.

Therefore, after a few years, and under the encouragement of others—including my wife—I have aimed to wrestle through some of these questions in a more public manner. This has greatly helped me, and our prayer is that it may prove useful to others in some small way. But the truth is, writing like this is not easily accomplished without violating certain sacred spaces for my family. So, while we have been persuaded that allowing readers to know a certain amount of our personal struggle might prove helpful, this book will not be an autobiography, though we must confess from the start it is deeply personal. How can we think and wrestle through these challenges in any other way? It is necessarily personal.

Through these years we have wrestled in various ways with suffering, grief, and loss. We've had to ask hard questions about God, his will, ourselves, and relationships. We have wrestled with issues of identity and purpose. These have not been easy years, and there are no simple answers. But this journey has been our story; our existence lived with and before God.

I begin with this brief snapshot of our lives not because I aim to write a story about us but to admit up front that this subject of suffering is not hypothetical for our family. Nor do I imagine that it is hypothetical for you. Consequently, the reflections that follow do, in some way, reflect our own family's wrestling through the ravages and emotional toll of physical suffering. However, besides this personal introduction to the book, you will not find lots of narratives about my own family, although stories of others who entrusted their experiences to me are spread throughout the book. It should be clear as you read, that this book is not written in a detached manner, because it is inevitably personal to my family and me. Yet let me be clear: my purpose here is neither autobiographical nor simply to tell powerful stories about individuals who struggle: this book is a *theological* and *pastoral* meditation. We will be exploring truths about God and ourselves. We will have to do some hard thinking that might stretch us, but I believe the payoff is well worth it: all our reflections on God inevitably come with pastoral and very personal implications. Thank you for entering in with me.

PART I

THE STRUGGLE

1

HARD THOUGHTS ABOUT GOD

*Not that I am (I think) in much danger of ceasing
to believe in God. The real danger is of coming to believe such
dreadful things about Him. The conclusion I dread is not "So there's
no God after all," but "So this is what God's really like.
Deceive yourself no longer."*

C. S. LEWIS, *A GRIEF OBSERVED*

*The LORD is near to the brokenhearted
and saves the crushed in spirit.*

PSALM 34:18

*As the bridegroom rejoices over the bride,
so shall your God rejoice over you.*

ISAIAH 62:5

This book will make no attempt to defend God. I will not try to justify God or explain away the physical suffering in this world. Instead, I wrestle with nagging questions about our lives, our purpose, and our struggles. How should we live in the midst of this pain-soaked world? How do we relate to the God whose world this is?

If you are looking for a book that boasts triumphantly of conquest over a great enemy or gives a detached philosophical analysis that neatly solves an absorbing problem, this isn't it. Instead, this book aims to invite you into a larger conversation, a conversation greater than my family, and a struggle bigger than your pain and doubt. For while our pain, or the suffering of those we love, may cause us to feel isolated, these challenges remind us that we are actually part of the much larger stream of humanity. A stream that is all too familiar with physical pain.

ADMITTING THE COMPLEXITY OF PAIN

As a result of wrestling with her own suffering, or "affliction" as she called it, philosopher and political activist Simone Weil wrote that such experiences have three dimensions that cannot be forgotten: physical, psychological, and social.[1] She emphasizes the importance of solidarity, the danger of isolation, and the crippling effects of despair that threaten those in pain. Her instinct to approach suffering in a way that attempts to weave together these various dimensions of our lives appears correct to me.[2]

Physical suffering often affects how we relate to God and others. For example, when a person's body is completely worn out from physical pain, he or she can perceive God as cruel. Talk of God's kindness can ring hollow, or worse, it can sound like a nauseating joke. The condition of our bodies does influence how we understand God and his ways. If bright lights or loud noises trigger chronic migraines for some people, wouldn't they hesitate to join worship services that use those features? Avoiding bright lights and pulsating music may not testify to their lack of spirituality but to their survival instincts. A thundering organ may cultivate reverence for some, but it might foster painful physical reactions for others. Pain in our body often influences how we relate to others. While avoiding certain worship services because of physical reactions may appear irreligious to people who enjoy those services, this impression fails to understand the challenges of unrelenting discomfort.

One man who suffers chronic pain explained his common struggle on Sunday mornings at church: "I feel guilty for having to sit during 'praise' time. I know how it can look. I don't have any visible physical 'condition.' So, in addition to the physical pain that I am having to endure while trying to worship God, I am often wrestling with my own desire to not appear 'irreligious.'" What some may imagine as signs of cool aloofness may in fact be acts of self-preservation and cries of despair. But we must, as Simone Weil urges us, remember how the social, psychological, and physical are woven together, mindful of how these circumstances also inform our relationship to God. These kinds of difficulties can roll over us like waves of the sea, creating particular and often awkward challenges for the believer and the church.

Limits are part of the everyday life of those with chronic pain. Sufferers may have to choose between a friend's engagement party and grocery shopping because they don't have the stamina to do both.[3] This doesn't make them antisocial. It doesn't mean they are unloving. Their physical suffering places stringent limits on them every day. Limits that isolate and exhaust.

As we examine our suffering, we must do our best to maintain a holistic perspective. We must not pit the body against the spirit, the mind against the heart, the individual against the community. For our struggle is not ultimately with a single side of suffering but with how it affects us in our totality: from our relationships to our faith, from our bodies to our hope, from our mourning to our love. Central to the complexity of our pain is how it can affect our view of God.

TEMPTED TO THINK ILL OF GOD

Christians, perhaps even more than those without faith in a personal and loving God, can feel not just alone but abandoned during times of difficulty. It is one thing for sufferers to cry out to the great Unknown, echoing the unsettling words of Stephen Crane:

A man said to the universe:

"Sir, I exist!"

"However," replied the universe,

"The fact has not created in me

A sense of obligation."[4]

Yet for the saint who confesses the personal God of Abraham, Isaac, Jacob, and Mary, such moments of despair can bring the fear of divine indifference, rejection, or judgment.

One of the most powerful temptations Christians face as they go through suffering is, to borrow a phrase from John Owen, to have "hard thoughts" about God.[5] By "hard thoughts" this Puritan theologian does not have in mind our honest questions that naturally arise amid struggles. We all have honest questions as we stand before God: *Why? How come? What does this mean? When will it end?* Such questions are not only understandable but healthy. Despite widespread misperceptions, Christian spirituality is not stoicism. Heartfelt cries and existential questions operate at the core of healthy theology, and suppressing them is more hurtful than a confession of ignorance. We will discuss this later when we get to the role of longing and lament. But what Owen has in mind is different, which is why these might be called "temptations" rather than merely honest struggles.

Whether first fostered from painful childhood experiences, heavy-handed preaching, or something else, we often imagine God in deeply problematic ways.[6] When experiences of physical suffering persist, it is all too common to find ourselves plagued by distorted perceptions of God, making him appear tyrannical or even demonic. Such "hard thoughts" are temptations because they can lead us to ultimate despair and away from communion with the loving Lord. They are temptations because our suffering and struggle entice us to think ill of God, to imagine him cruel and brutish. As Owen comments, we are "apt to have very hard thoughts of him,—to think he is always angry, yea, implacable; that it is not for poor creatures to draw nigh to him."[7] Such hard thoughts are destructive because they hide God from us, running counter to how the Father actually views his children:

> The Lord takes nothing worse at the hands of his [children], than such hard thoughts of him, knowing full well what fruit this bitter root is like to bear,— what alienations of heart,—what drawings back,—what unbelief and tergiversations [i.e., turning one's back] in our walking with him. How unwilling is a child to come into the presence of an angry father![8]

My wife describes feeling at times that God has more important things to deal with than one woman's pain. The needs of a suffering world require his full attention, and she just needs to toughen up. Such thoughts, as she would say, are incorrect and only drive the sufferer to isolation from God. But sufferers commonly find these thoughts creeping in, twisting their image of the divine. God's concern about such hard thoughts arises not because he cannot answer our questions or becomes defensive. No, they concern God because they keep us far from him.

This is the frame of mind that isolates us, distorting our image of the Creator and keeping us from knowing his compassion. Thus the sufferer, instead of seeing the Father, whose whole inclination toward us is love, mercy, and desire to commune with his children, sees in his place a false image of an angry, distant, austere being who can never be satisfied or happy. These false perceptions of the sufferers "are apt to impair and weaken their love towards him and delight in him."[9] When these misconceptions take hold, they throw cold water on the small embers of our love for God.

How can believers tossed and blown by the storms of life *not* succumb to false images of God? This question requires that we deepen our view of who God actually is and thus leave behind our own fears and the conceptual baggage about God we have casually acquired. Owen reinforces the claim that God, instead of being a harshly demanding and disappointed accountant in the sky, is in fact our own Father who, in his delight, always keeps a near and tender presence:

> Is there any thing possible more endearing to the heart of a creature than to hear such a testimony as that, Zeph. 3:17, concerning the stability of the love of God, and its excellency, "The LORD thy God in the midst of thee is mighty; he will save, he will rejoice over thee with joy; he will rest in his love, he will joy over thee with singing?" God's resting in his love towards his saints fixes their souls in their love to him.[10]

Our legitimate dislike of shallow sentimentality about God raises our suspicion about this vision of God joyfully singing over his people. Yet these words come not from a sappy greeting card or a people-pleasing pastor but from the deep prophetic soul of Zephaniah, who knew God's judgment on corruption and God's concern over issues of injustice and neglect; he also knew of God's faithfulness to his people and the hope that it held out. Our inclination to dismiss this imagery of God singing as meaningless sentimentality is not a sign of our willingness to be realistic but of pre-conceptions of God informed by unbiblical impulses, such as those acquired from bad television and sloppy preaching. Take careful note of the places that the Bible's descriptions of God make us uncomfortable, and ask why they do so. These observations reveal broader problems in our thinking and attitudes. These are the places to dig in and rebuild.

Zephaniah's words call us to reconsider what we imagine God to be like, to ask how it might be possible that he rejoices over us with singing. Taylor is a boy who has been exceptionally empathetic since his earliest years. At twelve his heart remained tender and sensitive but also vulnerable to other people's pain and sadness. One Sunday after watching just the first part of *The Fellowship of the Ring*, the preteen awoke around midnight because of the frightening images of shadowy horsemen and twisted orcs that now flitted through his imagination. He saw Frodo's fear and darkness hovering over the land. He wept. He tried to console himself, to bring himself courage, but apparently it would not come.

Finally, upon hearing the tears his father, Michael, went upstairs in the middle of the night. Michael prayed, he rubbed his son's back, and then he slowly moved toward the door. When his father tried to leave, comfort and sleep also instantly departed from Taylor. So the father returned, and this time he simply sat over his boy and sang softly. Evidently as long as he sang, the boy was able to sleep. As soon as he would try to cease from his serenading, the boy awoke. So the father stayed, he sang, and he eventually just nestled in next to the boy. The father didn't sleep much that night, but the child fell into a deep slumber, both calm and grateful simply for the presence that was beside him and the voice that hung over him.

How is it that the heavenly Father, who is consistently described as "full of compassion," might not show such concern for his daughters and sons? Why do we find it so difficult to embrace Zephaniah's tender image? Isaiah similarly drew on such imagery, only changing the metaphor from a Father singing over his children to the promise of a husband delighting in his wife: "As the bridegroom rejoices over the bride, so shall your God rejoice over you" (Is 62:5). Why does this make us so uncomfortable?

How does God look upon us in our weakness, even in our sin? Is God really angry or wrathful with us, his children? His bride? What picture of

God is really warranted by the Scriptures? How do these passages like Zephaniah 3:17 and Isaiah 62:5 intersect our own experience? How can we then deal with the "hard thoughts" that tempt us, especially in our suffering? How do we develop a profound and affectionate trust of God rather than a sense of alienation? Our journey is to learn why such hard thoughts don't reflect the triune God. Our hope is to learn to hear him singing over us, to trust his presence in the middle of the pain. Some will immediately object that this is wishful thinking based on a few obscure verses here and there. However, we will see that we are not talking about a few scattered biblical texts but diving into the heart of the gospel, the heart of the good news discovered in the Messiah. Only here will we unquestionably discover the very heart of God.

To understand God and his relationship to our pain, we will need to examine the case of Jesus of Nazareth, a man who walked the dusty roads of Galilee over two thousand years ago. Only by listening to his words and by following the movement of his life, death, resurrection, and ascension might our very human struggle be seen in different light. Because he was and is God's revelation of himself to us, it only makes sense to start there. In this endeavor it is to be hoped that our view of the God of heaven and earth will deepen beyond our current understanding. But to see Jesus clearly we need to stop defending our preconceived notions of who God is.

If you are plagued by "hard thoughts" of God, don't give up. No easy answer will suffice, and no pill can make everything instantly well. Still, I hope that what follows will give genuine encouragement and glimpses into the heart of God. Along the way we will be reminded not only how much we need God but how much we need his people—we need each other. This, as we will see, informs how we might start to address questions about our suffering.

WHERE WE ARE GOING:
OVERVIEW OF THE REST OF THE BOOK

My goal is not to explain away human suffering on the one hand or the goodness of God on the other. Instead, we continue on a journey of faith, an encounter with the living God, our Creator and Redeemer. This is the story of the God who is more holy than we can imagine and more near than we dare believe. This is the God whose perfections provoke awe, yet whose movement of condescension frightens us in its humility. This is the story of

Emmanuel, the story of the gospel, and the story of how those who know this Lord can live amid the rubble, the dark questions, and the daunting fears. This is the story of what it means to be a creature living with hope in a broken world—not a hypothetical world but this world, filled with beauty and tears, with laughter and ache.

As we proceed, I hope to keep things more manageable by narrowing our discussions with two assumptions. First, this book specifically addresses *Christians* who suffer, and not the more general—and profoundly legitimate—questions about universal human suffering. While I will be speaking of suffering as experienced by Christians, I believe it relates to all people who roam the earth. In this world the reality of suffering afflicts all humanity; in fact its universal nature serves as a great equalizer. We all share the experience of suffering. Yet, since I do not aim to solve the problem of suffering but to talk about how a Christian might live in the midst of it, I will keep Christians as my primary audience.

Second, the suffering discussed here will normally mean the *suffering associated with serious illness or physical pain*.[11] Various hurts and difficulties often arise from this form of suffering. Physical pain normally affects us in holistic ways, from our emotions to our relationships, from our work to our leisure, from our private lives to our public engagements. All of those things are relevant to properly addressing suffering associated with physical pain. We will ask, What does it look like for the Christian, the saint, to go through the valley of such distress? I hope and believe that this book has application for dealing with all sorts of suffering and not merely the physical variety: many who have heard some of this material have let me know that while I focus on suffering associated with physical pain, there is real relevance for Christians in different situations (e.g., raised in an abusive home). My prayer is that this book will prove helpful to many, whatever form of suffering they might be enduring. Nevertheless, to keep this book shorter and more focused, the scope of the conversation here is intentionally limited. Therefore, while I will keep in mind larger issues related to various forms of suffering (e.g., injustice inflicted on us by hostile agents, etc.), I will focus on particular challenges associated with physical pain. Also, by approaching this topic through the particular lens of bodily suffering, thus emphasizing our physicality, I believe our understanding of the Christian story may take on fresh meaning and power.

In the chapters that follow we will look at the limitations of easy answers and the tension between our longings for peace and our laments that something is wrong. Next, we explore what it means to be embodied creatures and what this tells us about ourselves, our expectations, and even what kind of relationship we might expect with the Creator. Doubts about our body's value remain a significant stumbling block to genuine Christian spirituality, and this misunderstanding is often intensified by debilitating pain. We then turn to the strangeness of God as displayed in Jesus of Nazareth. Only by looking to this man can we reorient our experience of suffering in a way that is truly Christian.

We will go on to see that those who are part of the body of Christ live life together, a life of faith, hope, and love. Here we discover a pattern for Christian discipleship that allows for genuine struggle, communal support, and transformative affection. We wrestle and rest in this community. Next, I offer some reflections on the place of pain and confession. As surprising as it may seem, confession becomes a particularly life-giving necessity for those with physical pain: here confession and the community come together, drawing us back to Christ. Finally, I conclude with some particular pastoral reflections that I hope will prove practical to those who suffer or are caregivers. To understand how all of this works together, however, we must cover a fair amount of terrain. Like a rewarding view from the top of a mountain, we have to climb the trail to get there and marvel at the beauties of the mysteries along the way.

2

DON'T ANSWER WHY

Most people die of the cure, not the disease.

Molière, *The Miser and Other Plays*

You have kept count of my tossings;
put my tears in your bottle.
Are they not in your book?

Psalm 56:8

The world is everything that is the case. . . .
Whereof one cannot speak, thereof one must be silent.

Ludwig Wittgenstein, *Tractatus Logico-Philosophicus*

I need not debate the realities of evil and suffering in this world: who can deny them? Nor will I argue for God's existence, since I assume this to be the case. I do not think we must choose between affirming the reality of God and confessing the pain of human suffering. We can work forward from the view that both are true. We can acknowledge the struggle of being a follower of Yahweh, the creator of heaven and earth, and having to deal with suffering as it is: real, tragic, and heartbreaking.

To give a partial explanation of why I start at this point, we can take half a step backward to ask why using theodicy (defending God's goodness) in circumstances of suffering is less than useful. This exercise will hopefully improve our ministry to those who suffer.

WHEN PHILOSOPHERS SHOULD BE SILENT

Gottfried Wilhelm von Leibniz (1646–1716) famously wrote a treatise titled *Theodicy*, in which he aimed to reconcile God's perfection with the intractable problem of evil. Theodicies normally attempt to make sense of the apparent tension between human misery and the existence of an all-powerful, wholly good, and wise deity: how can there be so much pain in this world if such a God exists?

Writing in the years after the horrific Lisbon earthquake of 1755, in which tens of thousands died in just three days, Voltaire wrote *Candide* as a parody of philosophies that tried to make sense of pain. His infamous character Dr. Pangloss reflects Leibniz's philosophy. Despite endless injustices and the most gruesome situations happening all around the characters, Pangloss's constant mantra is that this is the "best of all possible worlds." The novel made Leibniz's theodicy look naive at best and cruelly absurd at worst.

While the philosopher may convince his audience that the problem of suffering does not logically rule out the existence of a wholly good God, that view remains a great distance from the reality of faith in the God and Father of our Lord Jesus Christ and the foot of the cross. Only from that location at Golgotha will all of these questions be transformed, and only from that position might a truly Christian "explaining of the ways of God" occur.

Even if we had in hand a theodicy that made sense, such dispassionate philosophical explanations leave us empty when we walk in the fire and ashes of genuine suffering.[1] While there is a time to carefully dissect these philosophical problems, that time is not normally with those who are suffering. Such clinical reflections don't tend to help but often cause more pain to those who mourn and ache. Theodicies don't naturally belong in the home of the afflicted, even if they do need careful attention in the classroom.

Alvin Plantinga, one of the great American philosophers in the last seventy-five years, is also a Christian. He has written extensively on knotty intellectual challenges associated with faith, evil, human agency, and the like. While he insists that the problem of evil cannot preclude or even render improbable the existence of God, he also recognizes the difference between a problem in thought and a problem in life. "Of course, suffering and misfortune may nonetheless constitute a problem for the theist," but not a logical problem. Instead, the theist faces an existential and religious difficulty.[2]

When a person faces grave sorrow in their own life or in the life of one they dearly love, Plantinga affirms that it can be profoundly difficult even for the believer to maintain a proper posture before God. "Faced with great personal suffering or misfortune, he may be tempted to rebel against God, to shake his fist in God's face, or even to give up belief in God altogether." When suffering provokes a rejection of God, the issue is not primarily intellectual but "a problem of a different dimension. Such a problem calls, not for philosophical enlightenment, but for pastoral care."[3] The questions people ask amid suffering may have the same wording as academic problems, but they are not the same questions; the subtext here is not theoretical curiosity but guilt, isolation, fear, and often a distorted view of God.

Indeed, when problems move from the hypothetical to the personal, they look and feel different. John S. Feinberg had for years devoted himself to a thorough philosophical and theological inquiry into the problem of evil.[4] Yet his understanding of the problem changed when his wife was diagnosed with Huntington's chorea, a rare genetically transmitted disease that involves premature deterioration of nerve cells within the brain. Over time, the disease creates both psychological and physical trauma as the afflicted one loses control of certain bodily movements, often faces depression, and experiences severe memory loss. Eventually it can result in hallucinations and even paranoid schizophrenia. To make matters worse, Huntington's could be passed genetically to their children.

His meticulous answers and well-researched publications offered no real comfort to him in the face of this news and the difficult life they began to face. Careful arguments about human agency, contingency, and evil did not give hope or rest. It was not that his previous philosophical efforts were unwise or wrong, but they did not reach the places of his and his family's pain. The theories could not plumb the depths of human sorrow. They needed pastoral care. They needed the quiet presence of others around them. They needed glimpses of God in his goodness and love, truths often only made believable through personal tenderness and gentle grace extended to them by others. This family needed the warmth of God's presence rather than the cool calculations of logical deductions.

HOW THE CHURCH RESPONDS TO SUFFERING

John Swinton, in his excellent book *Raging with Compassion*, observes that these attempts to justify God and explain evil or suffering are largely irrelevant to those in the midst of suffering and can actually cause more problems than they solve. Justifications of God had their origins in an Enlightenment context that held rationality and science to have the highest values and orthodox Christian ideas to have little or none. In such an atmosphere, even Christians were tempted to defend God on Enlightenment terms.[5] This framework allowed all questions, but it also put its own requirements on answers it considered to be valid. Prominent among these were the assumptions that (1) the critical scholars were working from a neutral point of view, (2) educated European standards of reason and justice were both universal and clearly apprehended by the critical scholars, and (3) they were capable of rising above and comprehending all the relevant elements of the problem to formulate a coherent set of applicable universal rules. Such a framework profoundly skewed how one approached these questions.

Both testaments of the Bible ask and address deep and difficult questions about pain, suffering, the apparent triumph of evil, and the apparent absence of God in times of stress. We see this most especially in the psalms. They contain multiple examples of lament and struggle, and orthodox Christian theology follows that path. Augustine and others wrote extensively about the presence of evil in a world governed by a good and gracious sovereign Lord. Yet their approach was not from a position of supposed neutrality or assuming that God was no more than another piece of a puzzle, subject to human judgment. They approached the question from a starting point of faith, and the problem for them was deeper and more difficult because of that. Alasdair MacIntyre, for example, wonders why these issues were not previously seen as "an obstacle to belief," even though these Christians saw the problem of evil as clearly and deeply as any Enlightenment freethinker.[6] The difference between an Augustine and a Voltaire is not that the believer was credulous or superficial and the unbeliever a more rigorous thinker. The eighteenth century did not discover new pieces to the puzzle that were unknown to the fourth century. The difference now was that expectations and assumptions were reshaped. Reasons were demanded and justifications required because the culture decided that they could put God under the microscope along with everything else. It is not that pre-Enlightenment approaches were perfect and without shortcomings. Yet a significant shift seems to occur after the Enlightenment, which made it difficult for us to confess the limits of our understanding—if we don't know something, there *must* be a discoverable answer. Post-Enlightenment Europe decided that it could even fully understand transcendental realities in contemporary terms and sensible formulas. But the psalms, which are full of struggle, do not point us to answers and formulas. Hope? Yes. Answers? No. The psalms orient us to God. Our hope is in him who made and redeemed heaven and earth, not in our own intellectual acuity.

In the past, believers fully understood that evil and suffering existed. It was their place, as the people of God, to resist the evil when they could, and to mourn and lament the brokenness that they could not overcome. In fact, as we will see, their willingness to lament and hope amid their trouble was part of their answer to the suffering. The problem of evil was not so much a philosophical difficulty for pre-Enlightenment believers but a "practical challenge for the Christian community."[7] How do we live in God's compromised world? Ancient Christians responded with a set of practices and ways of living together with grace, solidarity, and promise amid the pain. These ways were not academic answers, but they were answers all the same. Different questions are being asked. The question we usually focus on is, why does evil exist? You can employ a theory for that. If the question instead is, how do we live?, then theories don't really satisfy. Practices—not theories—become most relevant.

In the third chapter of Job, for example, the sufferer responds to his situation with heartfelt lament. And his lament is not in isolation but in the context of his closest relationships, namely, with his wife and friends. In their presence he turns this lament toward God in a way that shows his ultimate trust in his Creator-Redeemer. The other laments we read in the Scriptures present this same combination of detailed realism regarding discomfort, pain, and complex fears, and the conviction that God is present, powerful, wise, and good. They are as convinced that this is the God they have to deal with as they are of the reality of their suffering. They believe in a God who is not only holy but whose holiness is always characterized by compassion and grace; these attributes thoroughly define one another and are never in opposition. They see God not as removed from the earthly details of their lives but intimately and interestedly involved in them. Having such a worldview, they see it as a matter of course that lament is so often a response to suffering.

With the Enlightenment, Christians were often seduced into treating God not as their loving Father and covenant-keeping Lord but as a mental construct. Those Christians who accepted the abstract framework for discourse assumed by unbelievers (like Voltaire) lost the ground of their own proper theology, namely, the concrete invasion of history by this particular God. This framework, like a distorting lens, reshaped how people saw God and evil. When guided by the need for justifications and answers, growing Christian attempts to "explain the ways of God" tended to foster distortions, especially in pastoral situations. Swinton highlights three of the most common consequences.[8] First, such explanations, by trying to integrate evil as part of the world, often end up justifying or rationalizing evil rather than confessing and naming it. Too often when Christians start to defend God in this way, they end up calling evil or suffering "good." Second, when people mistake theodicies for pastoral care, the voice of the sufferer is often silenced. Rather than offering the comforting presence of compassionate listening, these abstractions smother the wounded with useless and often inaccurate explanations. This works a form of violence against the hurting one, whether unintentional or not. And finally, these attempts to justify and explain *why* the evil has occurred can actually become evil in themselves, promoting further suffering rather than providing genuine comfort.

How often have well-intentioned ministers or friends tried to explain away a particular death, disease, or worse by an uninformed appeal to God's purposes? Do any of us really know why a particular event happens? Claims to provide the reason for a specific experience of suffering abound: divine discipline, for the purpose of church renewal, to bring a watching nurse or neighbor to salvation, or to foster personal humility. Unfortunately, all these claims are made without true knowledge of exactly why something is happening. Even if these suggestions contain an element of truth, we are not in a position to unpack the mind of God regarding such mysteries. What happens if the nurse who professes faith later abandons that faith or the apparent church renewal quickly fades away? Resting our faith on such connections can actually prove to be far more hazardous than most people realize. Such explanations assume that some good outcome can nullify or justify the pain, but this is not so. A tragedy is still a tragedy; pain is still pain, even if some insight is gained in the process. We may hope that God has reasons for allowing suffering in his world, but that is very different from thinking we have access to those reasons or can understand why a particular experience of suffering is taking place.

DON'T EXPLAIN, BUT DO LISTEN AND LOVE

Pastors and friends are not called to explain away the pain or to try to give moral lessons for why a particular event is happening. We simply are not privy to such information. While God can and does bring about good through our suffering, that is not the same thing as knowing why God allows it. Nor is it the same thing as saying that God thinks our suffering is good. If we believe that God thinks our physical suffering is essentially good, we misunderstand the Creator and Redeemer, and we are brought to the temptation of having hard thoughts about God, believing him to be more like a dispassionate scientist or a cruel tyrant rather than a loving Father. While it is true that amid our fallen world God can and does work through our pain and suffering, that does not mean he delights in our discomforts. And it does not mean that we can substitute theoretical reasoning for justified lament.

All of us will face times of physical illness, disease, and pain. In such times we do not normally need philosophical axioms—as important as they can be to legitimate philosophical investigation.[9] We need words and ears that understand suffering, that can handle honesty, vulnerability, and questions, and that know how to bring the wounded to sustaining faith, hope, and love.

To understand God and his work in our lives better, we need to recognize and deal with our limits, naiveté, and the complexity of human suffering. This includes recognizing that our post-Enlightenment culture has distorted our view of God and reassessing what it means to walk through a painful world with a loving Lord. We will need to learn afresh what it means to point people to Jesus and his kingdom, but not as a slogan, not as a quick fix, not as a superficial answer. We must point to the profound and redemptive compassion of Jesus, the Son of God, who healed the sick and entered into genuine human suffering and even death by crucifixion. His life, death, and resurrection must continually reshape how we view the cosmos, our place and even our suffering within it, and the God we believe in.

DEVELOPING PASTORAL SENSITIVITY
AND THEOLOGICAL INSTINCTS

This book aims to provide reflections that will prove helpful to some who are wrestling with personal pain and suffering, but it also hopes to offer counsel to those who are walking alongside loved ones who are in the midst of the storm.

Loving well those facing the great trials of life requires Christians to develop both *pastoral sensitivity* and *theological instincts*. Empathy and orthodoxy both matter. Benevolence and truth are meant to nourish one another, not to serve as two distinct options. When tenderheartedness and conviction are together, they bring life, but separated they can be disastrous. Discovering a perfect balance that allows a person to know the "right" response to every challenge is not the goal. Rather, Christians are those who experience the "faith and love that are in Christ Jesus" even as they cherish "the good deposit" handed down to them from the prophets, apostles, and through the ages (2 Tim 1:12-14). We cannot rest in the good news of Christ if we devalue the truths of sacred Scripture, but we also need to value experience if those truths are going to be applied and understood in any meaningful way.

Rightly understood, *doing* theology is more often like farming than it is like stacking doctrinal bricks. Theology is lived; it is not regimentally constructed. Like a gardener studying the soil over many years and watching the clouds in the sky each day, the Christian seeks to develop wise theological instincts so they may be able to know when to plant, when to uproot, when to water, and when to rest. Every season brings new challenges and fresh promises. Cultivating applied theological instincts is therefore inevitably a bit messy. You have to get your hands in the mud. Gardeners must discover the kinds of things that affect their crops' growth—often a plant's health depends on much more than the untrained observer realizes. Does the garden need more protection from the sun? What is in the soil? Funny enough, sometimes you discover more nitrogen may be needed—more manure! Are there rocks buried where the roots need expansion? Is there too much rain? Too little? Are there ravenous animals around who will eat whatever growth occurs as fast as it shows up? How might environmental factors shape the plant, for better or worse? We need to recognize different seasons, different threats, and different possibilities, and then act according to that information. To prepare a garden always the same, never asking about changing conditions, is not only naive but risks losing your harvest in the long term.

To develop a theology of suffering, we can't simply talk about suffering! Doctrines from various places—sometimes on the surface appearing un-related—need to be explored. Consider pain and the fall? Yes. But consider the goodness of creation. Consider individual fears? Yes. But consider the metaphysics of the community as well. Reflect on resurrection and hope? Absolutely. But also confess the cross, tragedy, and struggle.

Deliberately developing our theological instincts is deeply valuable, for it can help illumine the dark paths we find ourselves walking down. Paths need to be traveled, images need to be considered, songs need to be sung, silence needs to be observed. God must be present, sat with, listened to, and engaged. This takes us back to pastoral sensitivity.

Only when we begin to see that theology is not merely about repeating back answers but instead more like caring for a garden can we care well for others. Good gardeners have been trained to pay attention to the soil in their hands and not just the instructions in a book. From the book they have learned about soil, what is needed, what to add, and how to care for it. But in the end, nothing can replace examining the dirt itself, for no two patches of the land are the same.

Each person is coming from a different circumstance, with specific chal-lenges and needs, with individual strengths and temptations. Part of loving well is figuring out what response is needed and appropriate in a given cir-cumstance (see Jude 22-23). This is where theological instincts and pastoral wisdom come together.

To be pastoral does *not* mean earning money for working in a church. Throughout Christian history God's people have always been thankful for those with pastoral gifts among them—whether women or men, ordained or not, young or old, rich or poor. *Pastoral* in this sense refers to the ability to give wise counsel, to know how to love well, provide necessary guidance, and in the end to help a fellow believer flourish under God's grace and love, even as they seek to love their neighbor and serve God's kingdom.

So, pastoral wisdom requires not merely theological knowledge but shepherding abilities. You need to know the sheep. You need to know the person or people you are dealing with. It may sound cliché, but if we could only get past the knee-jerk Christian reaction of one size fits all, we might really be able to care for people.

There is no theological replacement for knowing people, their problems, the complexities, and the stories. That doesn't mean you can't say anything in general, but it does mean there is a world of difference between reading a book about gardening and actually gardening. There is a world of difference between reading a book about caring for people and actually caring for people. To theologize well, we need to love well. We need to care about anthropology (the study of humans) and not just theology (the study of God). Pastoral wisdom and theological instincts must go together. They must serve one another.

Attempts at pastoral wisdom without developed theological instincts quickly dissolve into mere moralism or a psychological cul-de-sac. Theological ideas divorced from pastoral wisdom quickly become harsh or even tyrannical principles that lack concrete expressions of love and grace. Let's avoid choosing between these. Let's grow in our knowledge and love of God even as we grow in our commitment to understand and care for one another. Orthodox theology and compassionate concern always belong together.

3

LONGING AND
LAMENT

For God alone my soul waits in silence. . . .
For God alone, O my soul, wait in silence.

PSALM 62:1, 5

Psalms of lament allow us to speak from the darkest regions of the heart, where
our despair threatens to overwhelm us. In so speaking we do not exhibit a lack
of faith, but stand in a biblical tradition that recognizes that no part of life,
including the most hideous and painful parts, is to be withheld from God, who
loves us, who in Jesus Christ speaks the psalms of lament alongside us, and
who proclaims hope, when there can—at least for the time being—be no hope
in us. The Church would do well to recover this biblical practice of lamentation.

NANCY J. DUFF, "RECOVERING LAMENTATION AS A
PRACTICE IN THE CHURCH"

Man who is born of a woman
is few of days and full of trouble.
He comes out like a flower and withers;
he flees like a shadow and continues not.

JOB 14:1-2

Human history is a story of incomprehensible joy, stunning accomplishments, and life-giving relationships. But it is also a story of tedious days, devastating diseases, and broken bodies. We can walk on the moon, yet we have no words, no strength, and no answers for parents who have just learned that their child has leukemia. Life seems to have more deep valleys and long desert roads than shady alleys or grand boulevards. Physical limits, disease, heartbreak, and ultimately death come to all.

Our lives have both light and darkness, both magnificence and brokenness, but we are inclined to see only one side at any given time. When we are up, we neglect to consider our times of anguish; when we experience intense suffering, it is easy to see only darkness. Thus, those who are in a period of relative comfort can find it very difficult to connect with the grief of those around them, and indeed the well-being of a neighbor can deepen the grief of someone in pain. Life is not simply pain, but this life inevitably includes suffering, and to imagine otherwise is to flirt with the fantastical rather than to face the real.

In large part our deep longing is for rich and nourishing peace—what the ancient Hebrews called *shalom*—which makes our present suffering so difficult to bear. Not only do we have to suffer the pain itself but also the knowledge and frustration of its wrongness. So the world is not as it should be. It is *not* "good." We know that harmony between people, between humanity and the land, between our heads and hearts, between heaven and earth is not just an object of our desire but is good and true. This knowledge adds a bitterness to the brokenness of the world, emphasizing the difference between our expectations of the good and our experience of its absence. This sometimes results in relational breakdown as well. How often have marriages fallen apart after a grave illness strikes a child, or once vibrant friendships turned cold after one person is no longer able to be as active as the other?

This common human craving for shalom frequently surfaces most intensely in our darkest hours. Some claim such yearnings are simply wish projections we create, hopes cultivated to keep us sane while we suffer. Yet such a cynical view of human futility leaves us all open to despair, not just when we suffer but even when things are going well. Is there really no difference between shalom and chaos, between pain and relief? People all around the world and throughout history have not found it so hard to imagine that the human creature has a purpose, a *telos*. The genuine tastes of harmony and grace we sometimes experience appear to point beyond us to a larger narrative.

When we express our longing for lasting shalom but also confess its current transitory nature, a compelling story develops, one that makes sense of love and yearning without doing violence to the complexity of the current human condition. Rejecting both utopianism on the one hand and despair on the other leads us to what might be called defiant hope.

Love in this life inevitably involves suffering. Some people, realizing this, harden their hearts or choose some form of self-destruction. For example, couples who go through repeated miscarriages often struggle with crushing grief and disappointment. Sometimes people suggest that they not get their hopes up lest they be devastated yet again. "Protect your hearts," they are told. Yet protecting their heart only means that they steel it against hope and joy and make it fit to feel only disappointment and pain. That is calling them not to life but to death—such suggestions require them to slowly kill off their heart. So they risk, they yearn, they long, and they struggle. Why? Because they dare to love. Most who truly love others will at some point have their hearts join the chorus of lament in the human drama.

THE NECESSITY OF LAMENT

Laments rise to the heavens as a strange combination of complaint, grief, questions, confusion, desire for rescue, and expectation of divine faithfulness. Our great hope is that lament is not *all* there is to human experience. Nevertheless, any who have truly lived and loved must come to believe that lament is at least part of our existence. Only the idealistic and unloving belittle tears and sadness. Only the coolly detached never raise a complaint about the condition of things, including our broken bodies. If we never lament, then it is legitimate to wonder if we have ever truly loved. Biblically we discover that lament is a legitimate, even necessary, form of fellowship with God when we are in a place of pain. The Bible repeatedly affirms lament to be an honest and expected expression of our battle with the brokenness of ourselves and the rest of the world.

Our background, however, often inclines us to be uncomfortable with lament and mourning. This discomfort comes from various contributions of Western civilization and not from the Scriptures. Even when we face death, the last enemy, we in the West can reject expressions of grief at memorials as excessive or sacrilegious. Some even go so far as to call funerals "celebrations" and encourage people not to wear black.[1] Even those without any faith commitments occasionally speak of transcendent peace, future reunions, "better places," and new realms of love.[2] Well-meaning Christians sometimes suppress their dark anguish because of their belief in heaven, as if mourning and biblical hope were necessarily at odds, despite the historical Christian affirmation of the place of lament. As one of my self-described "bicultural" Christian friends explained, he really "prefers the Korean version of funerals and memorials to American ones. Wailing and heavy drinking seem much more in accord with what is happening inwardly." Many agree with his sentiment. One day while my wife and I lived overseas, we were walking home and heard the harrowing cries of those outside a hospital, wailing over the death of a loved one. Though there was some reason to believe these mourners were Christians, this was their response, culturally accepted and even expected. Our cultural sensibilities were shocked, but on reflection it seems a truer reflection of the soul's cry against the robber named Death. A simple verse telling them not to mourn like unbelievers will not do. Christians are different because of our hope in Christ, who has overcome death. But death is still an enemy, so grief and mourning are an appropriate and realistic response to the loss of the presence of our loved ones. We weep with those who weep.

While conducting his mother's funeral a number of years ago, Pastor Eugene Peterson was so overcome with the ugliness and pain of death that he broke down and wept uncontrollably in front of those who were gathered there. After finishing the service, he went into a side room in order to settle himself. His daughter also came and sat with him, crying and lamenting along with him. A few moments later a man he did not know entered the room and sat down next to him. He placed his arm around Peterson, muttered some "preacherish clichés" in a "preacherish tone" and then stepped out, seemingly confident that his platitudes had properly consoled this distraught man. After his unsolicited comforter had left, Peterson leaned over to his daughter and said, "I hope I've never done that to anybody." His daughter reassured him that he had not.[3]

To have healthy fellowship with God we must be honest and realistic about our circumstances and our reactions to them. To have a healthy emotional, spiritual, and mental life, we must be honest with ourselves. One truth about our lives is that we are broken; we inevitably encounter our own suffering and that of others, and eventually we die. How does our Lord teach us to respond to this? He teaches us hope, and within that hope we use lament to speak to God of the painful delay of peace. All laments ultimately go to God, with whom we wrestle and rest.

Unfortunately, this tendency to downplay lament has been the experience of an ever-growing number of people. Perhaps it is has been your experience. The real problem is that this devaluing of lament often betrays our failure to admit that our suffering is real and painful. Our failure to practice lament during such times may also display our inability to recognize that what happens to our bodies also affects our relationships.

The human experience requires lament, at least as long as we live in the current world as we know it.[4] Biblically there can be no question about the place and need of this practice—sin and sickness mean we must create space for genuine lamentation. Not because we despair but because we recognize the wounds of this world and of our hearts. God instructs us to bring to him our tears, our hurts, our confusion. Old Testament scholar Daniel J. Simundson reminds us of this scriptural tradition:

> The lament allows for honest interchange between humans and God, the freedom to admit even bad theology and hostile thoughts. The lament turns to God as the ultimate source of help and, in the typical lament form, ends with the assurance that God has heard and will save. The lament does not solve all of the sufferer's intellectual questions about the origin and meaning of the suffering, but does provide a structured way for the faithful to bring their suffering to God's attention and to cope with it.[5]

If we do not restore space for lament in our individual and corporate church life, our suffering will drive us not only away from others but away from God himself.

In contrast with frequent Western practice, the New Testament narratives in which physical death occurs exhibit intense lament and tears, even from Jesus. Hope does not rule out the need for mourning in our lives but rather demands it, because our hope itself tells us that our brokenness is wrong. Hope does not cause the widow to cease missing the warmth of her beloved lying next to her each night in bed. Hope does not answer all of our questions. Christian hope does *not* mean a cessation of lament, since these two often go together. We imagine this as a linear relationship, in which a person experiences sadness for a time and then graduates to hope (the binary option). Not so. Or we imagine that the heart is a set of scales with pain and suffering on one side and faith and hope on the other. The lamenter may be told that if they add more hope and faith, these things outweigh the darkness and tip the scales (see fig. 1). Such imagery is not only unhelpful, it is wrong and does violence against the souls of those who suffer. It has no place in the church.

Lament ⟵   ⟶ Hope

Figure 1. Common binary option

We struggle and mourn not only at the presence of death but also in response to its far-reaching effects. Grieving often arises as we deal with debilitating sickness, when bouts with mental illness create unnerving chaos and unsettle established relationships, or as chronic pain becomes the unwelcome companion of those we love. To mourn, whether over the brokenness of our bodies or over the injustices of this world, is not simply an option but an obligation.[6] Going through chemotherapy or the treatment of an autoimmune disease, the believer may consistently oscillate between lament and hope, with neither canceling the other out. In fact, people testify to moments when both joyful hope and jarring grief are simultaneously present. Often they dwell together in our hearts as strange bedfellows (see fig. 2). Such emotional complexity is partly what can be so difficult on marriages and friendships, since it is not always easy for the caregiver to relate to the hurting one amid their turbulence. In the psalms, lamentations often carry hope within them, but they remain heartrending expressions of crying out to God. Mourning is a Christian practice: blessed are those who mourn. Yet we do not simply mourn, but we lament, for in our lamentations we ask deep questions, face darkness, voice our frustrations, and cling to unrealized promises. My family has been part of a multiracial and intentionally cross-cultural church. The worship style of this church is strongly influenced by

African American gospel traditions. This worship style is a good example of deep lament that never loses its hold on Christ and hope. It affirms that hope cannot be seen and felt unless brokenness and pain are recognized first.

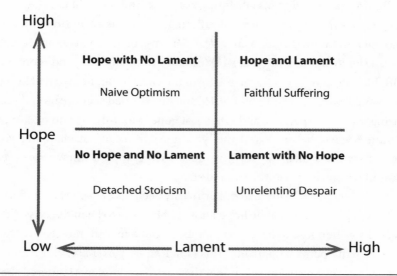

Figure 2. The hope-lament quadrant

When we choose not to lament, we harden our hearts. When we claim that the problems in this life are illusory, when we act as if all the wrongs from our physical pains or horrific injustices are insignificant—in short, when we try to wall ourselves off from suffering, we also wall ourselves off from others and from the God who tells us that this pain is a real, if temporary, fight that requires our attention. While certain stoic forms of spirituality encourage us to "accept," that has not actually been the Christian confession throughout the ages. Not all is good in this world. God, in his sovereignty, has recruited us into his war against darkness and death, and lament brings us back to our dependence on him in that fight. This lament does not undercut divine authority and care but rather beseeches the presence and comfort of God into the most wounded parts of our souls. Here I think of Carrie, who wrote an extended narrative to me a few years after losing her child in a most painful and devastating miscarriage. Even years after the devastating experience, she described the grace of lament in her life: "God fills up my emptiness with the promise of his presence. I was not and am never left alone in my lament." Lament takes one to our Father, and only in him can we discover hope in the midst of our most painful fears and frustrations.

Bob, a dear friend in his late fifties, asked if he might audit the class I was starting in a few days on faith and suffering.[7] Here was a faithful saint, elder, and pillar in his local church. To give you a sense of this man's heart, he once took a significant demotion at work in order to be able to spend more time with his wife and caring for members of the church. But he also had known real pain of various sorts in his life. He and his wife had spent years and years caring for elderly parents, and it had not gone smoothly. As you make your wedding vows, he once told me, you don't think about changing your mother-in-law's diapers. But love does such things. I knew there were painful family disappointments and struggles.

Even though his "pain" had not primarily been his own physical suffering, Bob explained to me that he hoped it would be okay to be in the class. Obviously I was honored to have him join us. About a month into class we took time to write personal laments. This is not an easy exercise, and it can be deeply painful. Sitting outside under the warm sun, students scattered about looking out over the Georgia valley from Lookout Mountain. Bob sat and started writing. About forty minutes later he came to me and handed me notes on a scribbled paper. He later gave me permission to share with you. Here is his "A Spontaneous Lament," which functions as a back and forth with his God:

> Why did my daughter's husband break her heart?
> > I know, little child
> Won't you tell me, Father?
> > I won't, my son
>
> Why does my wife have to live in pain?
> > I know little child
> Won't you tell me, Father? It would make it easier
> > It wouldn't, my son
>
> Why do parents have to bury their children? It isn't right
> > It isn't, little child
> Then get rid of death, Father
> > I am, my son

Why are your people abused, persecuted and killed? Can't you protect
    them?
   I can, little child
Then do something
   I did, my son

Why do my parents need to finish their lives in unrelenting misery? How is
    that merciful?
   It is, little child
Then I don't understand mercy
   You don't, my son

But it all hurts so much sometimes
   I know it does, little child
How do you know Father?
   I have felt all the pain of sin, my son

Can't you make it all stop?
   I can, little child
Then do it, Father
   I started 2000 years ago and will finish soon, my son

I believe you, Father, help my unbelief
   I love you, my son

Here Bob poured out his heart to our Father, who did not answer all his questions but took him to his Son. About three weeks after Bob wrote this lament, he got a call from his doctor while he was sitting at a Mr. T's Pizza Parlor. "Don't eat another bite," the physician asserted. In the following weeks Bob was diagnosed with pancreatic cancer. Now the pain was not his wife's or his daughter's, or anyone else's, but his own. I have watched Bob and his wife walk through this frightening time with courage and humor but also with a willingness to lament. This is not because they lack faith but because their faith is so real, so personal, so intimate. Where else can we turn with our questions, hurts, concerns, and longings? No one but the living God can fully handle our lamentations.

THE SHAPE OF OUR LAMENTS

God's good creation has been compromised, and to act as if it hasn't is offensive to the truthfulness of God. Not all is well in the land of the living. Yes, there is a danger of becoming so absorbed with our grief that we are tempted to believe there is nothing more than lament. I will speak of this later, but before I so quickly warn against endless despair, let's learn to allow our hearts and our communities the space to honestly struggle and ache before God and others. The songs of lament, which make up over 40 percent of the psalter, remind us that we can bring our questions and struggles to God himself. Consider some of the verses from Psalm 88:

> O Lord, God of my salvation;
>> I cry out day and night before you . . .
>
> For my soul is full of troubles,
>> and my life draws near to Sheol.
> I am counted among those who go down to the pit;
>> I am a man who has no strength,
> like one set loose among the dead,
>> like the slain that lie in the grave,
> like those whom you remember no more,
>> for they are cut off from your hand. (Ps 88:1-5)

Elsewhere such ache is vividly portrayed:

> My tears have been my food
>> day and night,
> while they say to me continually,
>> "Where is your God?" (Ps 42:3)

Jeanette Mathews, building on the work of those in the visual arts, argues that the idea of "framing" can help us better understand the place and practice of lament in the life of the people of God.[8] Mathews's "framing" functions like an actual frame used to hold a painting. Three things occur in this event. First, the frame *constrains* the artwork, actually setting limits or a boundary for the painting. This far and no further! The artwork cannot take over the house even as it is welcome to inhabit a space within the home. Second, the framing *heightens* our awareness of what we should be concentrating on and thus directs our contemplation. In this way the art is contrasted with what might be called normal life or the regular environment, as if the art takes us by the shoulders and shakes us awake, forcing us to look at what is right in front of our eyes. Without such a heightening of our senses, we risk becoming insensitive to what is all around us, including the presence of others and how they might be seeing the world. Third, the frame *clarifies* by helping to shape how we see the piece of art. We are drawn in, we focus, and then we see afresh.

Similarly, biblical laments offer a guide for our experiences. An ancient pattern is found in these biblical laments, encouraging us to actively cry out to God rather than merely become passively absorbed by the pain. Although not always proceeding in a neat fashion, the following elements are common in lament psalms:

- A cry out to God: "My God, My God, why have you forsaken me?"

- A complaint or voicing of the crisis that drives the poem: "Why are you so far from saving me, from the words of my groaning? . . . All who see me mock me."

- A petition in which remedy is yearned for: "Be not far from me, for trouble is near, and there is none to help."

- Often (though not always!) a claim of confidence in God: "All the ends of the earth shall remember and turn to the LORD."

- Often (though not always!) a commitment to praise God: "I will tell of your name to my brothers; in the midst of the congregation I will praise you."[9]

These poems and songs often contain elements of protest, frustration with God, or anger about the presence of injustice or ongoing suffering. Concern at God's lack of response is also common, sometimes wondering if God has nodded off ("Awake! Why are you sleeping, O Lord? Rouse yourself!" [Ps 44:23]). At other times, echoing the prayers of leaders like Moses (e.g., Ex 32:11-14), some lamentations debate with God, piling up arguments as if to convince Yahweh why action should be taken. Does Moses or the psalmist fail to believe in the sovereignty of God? Do they imagine somehow that God has limited cognitive functions and easily forgets? Certainly not. And yet they lament and wrestle with God. For these biblical leaders, God's presence and power does not eliminate their struggle but rather provides the ultimate context for it. In her reflections on the book of Lamentations, Kathleen O'Connor captures how these varied yet accepted patterns of wrestling with God serve the faithful:

> The point of lamenting is not to confess sin . . . but to name injustice, hurt, and anger. . . . Laments empower sufferers to speak for themselves. . . . Naming suffering before God reclaims human dignity and power that has been trampled and violated. . . . Laments are the beginning of action, a rejection of passivity, and so they can invert despair.[10]

These cries do not form a subversive antireligious voice but operate at the heart of the biblical canon among the prayers and songs of the people of God. They are part of their liturgy and worship. Laments are not just for individuals (e.g., Ps 3; 4; 13; 22; 31; 39; 57; 69; 71; 77; 139) but often reflect the cry of the community. For example, there are at least eleven community laments scattered throughout the Hebrew psalter (Ps 44; 60; 74; 79; 80; 83; 85; 90; 94; 123; 137).[11] The psalms not only offer praise to God and acknowledge his goodness but also ask if God has forgotten his people, if he remembers his promises and will yet display his compassion.

When contemporary churches cease to sing laments as part of their regular catalog of songs, instead only choosing happy or upbeat music, the people of God lose their ability to lament well: our muscles for godly mourning atrophy. We become ill-equipped to handle the pain that life throws at us. Without space for genuine lament, false veneers and bitterness easily take root, eventually bringing destruction in their wake. Suffering surprises and isolates once-active worshipers, often driving them away. When the homes of believers are hit by chronic pain or mental illness, they often find the contemporary church strangely unhelpful, even hurtful. A hurting family no longer fits the American Christian model of growth, happiness, and victory. When the church is robbed of its regular pronouncements, prayers, and songs of lament, then, like a shepherd distracted by the stars in the sky, it fails to protect and nourish the vulnerable sheep entrusted to its care. Rather than receiving special care and protection, the wounded believer is left alone to doubt and despair. The church that responds by entering their lament, however, participates in the healing that the wounded find at the feet of the compassionate Father. There we lay them; there we cry out with them; there we *together* long for healing and hope.

THE GOD OF OUR LAMENTS

Mary came to see me because she wanted to talk. The memories, grief, and ache were too much. She was overwhelmed by her own experiences and by the pain of others she had witnessed firsthand. Having grown up on a Native American reservation, she had seen and known a depth of sadness, despair, and darkness that haunted her many nights. We do not need to get into the details here, but one particular little girl's troubles were always before Mary. Eventually Mary's family brought the young girl into their home, cared for her, but also saw up close how painful dysfunction and abuse can be. What was Mary to do? She knew she should lament, but she was finding herself suffocated by all the grief and sadness.

Sehnsucht is a German word that people struggle to translate since it means "yearning, craving, or sensing something is profoundly wrong or missing." Some have noted how built into the idea of *sehnsucht* is a type of nostalgia; this form of sentimentality includes a feeling that not everything is right in this world, and so we long for another world. As Christians, we believe this feeling of *sehnsucht* and nostalgia is a longing for shalom.

As I listened to Mary I wondered what to say, and then it occurred to me. Mary was right: her lament was killing her. Suddenly, pieces of the puzzle began to make sense to me. If you could truly and fully lament, not just for yourself but for the world, it would kill you. Literally. Out of great pain Mary said to me, "I just don't have the time and energy for the laments. I've seen too much sorrow growing up." She was speaking the truth.

A full lament is deadly. We know this because when Jesus fully and truly enters into lament, it kills him.[12] He dies. But in his case his lament was not for himself but for others. He enters in so that our laments don't have to kill us. We will turn to this more in the coming chapters, but for now we need to be honest about the pain of lament and why we are inclined to avoid it. It hurts. And if we fully and completely felt the lament of this broken and sinful world, it would crush any and all of us. We know that because it crushed Jesus. But thanks be to God, this Jesus also rose from the depths of despair and from the grave. He rose and lives even now. For now, let us simply appreciate that we are allowed, even invited, to lament. Yet we must take those laments to God since they will not crush him.

Yahweh can absorb our frustrations; he doesn't fret before our questions; he is able to respond to our concerns. We must never forget "what ultimately shapes biblical lament is not the need of the creature to cry its woe, but the faithfulness of the God who hears and acts."[13] After voicing such laments—

dealing with everything from feelings of betrayal to persecution, from fear of death to a sense of being under judgment—our posture can then be changed. Instead of denying or dismissing the human struggle, lament reminds the worshiper of Yahweh's extraordinary care. "How precious is your steadfast love, O God! / The children of mankind take refuge in the shadow of your wings" (Ps 36:7). One does not need a shelter if there are no threatening elements. Amid violent storms or debilitating heat we become most conscious of our need for sanctuary.

> God is our refuge and strength,
>   a very present help in trouble.
> Therefore we will not fear though the earth gives way,
>   though the mountains be moved into the heart of the sea,
> though its waters roar and foam,
>   though the mountains tremble at its swelling. . . .
> The Lord of hosts is with us;
>   The God of Jacob is our fortress. . . .
> Be still, and know that I am God. (Ps 46:1-3, 7, 10)

Real threats are observed, real dangers swirl about. As part of his theology of the sovereignty of God, the psalmist knows God to be a refuge amid the chaos of struggle, pain, and confusion. Honest lament and mourning can allow us to receive hope and be open to God's presence in a way that appears impossible without such genuine acknowledgement of the questions and hurt. Again, the psalms give us not philosophical justifications for the presence of evil but instead join us in expressing heartfelt ache and confidence in God's presence. Hope comes to us not by denying or downplaying our pain but by acknowledging it before the God who abounds with compassion (Is 49:13).

Lament helps keep us sane amid physical suffering; it allows us to acknowledge real problems even as we hold out for the unrealized resolution. It affirms God's shalom even as it confesses our present trouble. As we wonder what it means to look to God amid our suffering, the only way we might keep our hope is to keep this larger, complex story of humanity in mind. Powerful, inventive, and delightful creatures that we can be, we also suffer and complain. We are never far from the dueling experiences of splendor and pain, triumph and tragedy. Lament allows us to embrace this tension without being swallowed up by it. It enables us to look for God's deliverance even as the sandstorm of life threatens and swirls.

We will only discover hope when we are ruthlessly honest about what lies between us and that hope. At least such truth telling is required if we are ever to know the true hope of the ancient Christian confession. The church denies the power of the gospel when it trivializes grief and belittles physical pain, overspiritualizing our existence in such a way as to make a mockery of the Creator Lord. Faithfulness to the gospel requires the Christian community to deal with the messiness of human grief. Biblical faith is not meant to provide an escape from our physical pain or to belittle the darkness of depression and death but rather invites us to discover hope and grace amid our struggle.

To be a truly human story—which is the only way we should understand the Christian story—means it must confess both grief and hope, sin and faithfulness, struggle and promise. We must learn to be truly honest with ourselves, with others, and even with God. Our theology requires it. Our stories demand it. Only with this kind of confession and lament are we finally in a position to capture a glimpse of the God who is, rather than the god we imagine him to be. Only then can we discover the scandalous grace of God so often spoken about but so seldom truly savored.

Some who experience chronic suffering see God not as a source of hope but of condemnation. Instead of compassion they see only judgment and indifference. What are we to think of God amid our suffering and as we struggle through our laments? It will prove necessary for us to reflect on the fact that humans are embodied, finite, and sinful creatures. Our finitude is not a sin, but the tyranny of sin and brokenness has affected our finitude, and this is especially seen as we experience suffering in our bodies. Only after we start to believe in God's commitment to us—including to our bodies—will we be ready to speak properly about Jesus. And then, turning to him we will gain not only a better understanding of ourselves but of God himself. What we discover may prove surprising.

4

EMBRACING OUR EMBODIMENT

What is man, that you make so much of him,
and that you set your heart on him?

JOB 7:17

For you formed my inward parts;
you knitted me together in my mother's womb.
I praise you, for I am fearfully and wonderfully made.

PSALM 139:13-14

Know that the LORD, he is God!
It is he who made us, and we are his;
we are his people, and the sheep of his pasture.

PSALM 100:3

When we are in serious or prolonged physical pain, it is easy to believe that our bodies are our chief problem. We struggle to believe that our physicality could have meaning, purpose, or some original good intent. This temptation to condemn or hate our bodies can be very strong indeed, and it has a long history in philosophy and theology. Yet to retreat from the body and focus only on some idea of a ghostly soul is to lose our way. While concentrating on the soul can sound spiritual and wise, it is sometimes anything but.

Contrary to some popular notions, the Christian faith strongly affirms the importance and goodness of our bodies. As a result, the Christian tradition sees sickness as a genuine problem worthy of both attention and lament rather than something to be ignored as meaningless. Only with a robust appreciation of our physicality can we properly understand how human relationships work and why bodily pain and personal interaction are intimately interconnected. This latter point will absorb our attention for the rest of this chapter.

OUR BODILY SELF

Who are you?

This simple question obviously requires a complex answer, and we specifically want to investigate what place our bodies have in that answer. We often start with a nonphysical idea about our identity (rationality, etc.), but even rationality involves our bodies. For example, to speak and breathe in rational communication, we need the air that moves through our throat and trachea into our lungs. To hear and understand requires the process of transmitted sound waves coming though the ear canal with vibrations that affect the bones in the middle ear, eventually received by tiny hair cells that are sound sensitive. Our neurological synapses enable us to remember where we live, what we believe, and who we love. All of these physical functions play an essential part in our ability to reason, our training of that ability, our self-perception, and our interaction with others. As concrete particular examples of humanity, we need our bodies to exist. They are hugely relevant to understanding not just *how* but also *who* we are. This becomes especially clear to those who lose any of these functions or other common physical abilities.

We are, of course, fully human even when one or more of our physical functions disappear. Various limitations are, by definition, part of creaturely life, so we should avoid the mistake of thinking that only complete and idealized physical function allows us to be human. Thomas Reynolds labels this mistake "the cult of normalcy" in his thoughtful discussion of disability.[1] Our bodies take different forms and have different capacities, and much of this is what marks us out as distinctive and meaningful creatures. In every degree of limitation our bodies have purpose and dignity, and concepts of humanity must affirm rather than belittle our physicality in order to be Christian concepts. Consequently, the way to live amid our physical pain and struggles is not to minimize our body's importance but to discover how God views our bodies.

Far too often in history, even within the church, our bodies have been treated with suspicion. Much of this suspicion has risen from non-Christian influences: for example, it was Plato, not Moses, who created the myth of the fall of souls, formerly free from physicality but then cast down into the troubles of bodily life.[2] It was Plato, not Paul, whose view is often summarized by the axiom, "The body is the prison-house of the soul."[3] Biblical narratives instead affirm the dignity of human bodies. Only when we work from that background can we understand, for example, what Paul and others mean by the dangers of the "flesh," by which they do not normally refer to our physicality but rather rebellion against God.

CREATED WITH BODY AND SOUL

God freely created all that is not God (e.g., Gen 1:1; Ps 33:6; 148:5; Jn 1:3; Col 1:16; Heb 11:3 [see 2 Macc 7:28]), and all of it was good.[4] From the lizard warming itself on the rock to the moon illumining the night, God made everything and repeatedly affirmed it all as good (Gen 1:4, 12, 18, 21, 25). This burst of creative energy and force reached a crescendo when "the LORD God formed the man of dust from the ground and breathed into his nostrils the breath of life, and the man became a living creature" (Gen 2:7). Joining the chorus begun by the deep roars of the beasts and the songs of the fluttering birds, this particular creature entered into the harmony of the rest of creation, and all was deemed "very good" (Gen 1:31). The earth and all that inhabited it were not embarrassing to the Lord of heaven but rather a delight to him, so much so that he made time for a sabbath (Gen 2:1-3; Ex 31:17). Taking satisfaction in his manifold work, he invites humans to enter into his rest and enjoy all his handiwork (Deut 5:12-14).

Man and woman are made out of dust and breath (Gen 2:7; see Ps 104:29), and thus they are as earthy as one can imagine. Yet humans are also set apart by the wise and loving Lord to care for and live in harmony with the rest of creation (Gen 1:28-31; 2:19-20). This man and woman, made in Yahweh's image and likeness (Gen 1:27), walked with God and were designed to enjoy companionship. The opening chapters of Genesis do not speak of this pair apart from their physicality. While they are not *merely* material things, neither do they have their being apart from their bodies made from the dust (see Gen 18:27; Ps 103:14; 1 Cor 15:45-49).

Unlike Plato's philosophy, the biblical presentation frames original human goodness within bodily existence, not apart from it. Our physicality was not a problem to be overcome but a gift essential to our existence. Regardless of how one works through the difficult issues related to body and soul, the Bible presents a unified picture of the human person.[5] Put differently, communion with God and others was always meant to take place in and through the body, not apart from it.[6] This was our created state; this will be our ultimate hope.[7]

The only thing in all of God's good creation not deemed good was Adam's isolation (Gen 2:18). Obviously no animal companion would be enough. Instead God forms a woman so that humankind would be both male and female. Now they could flourish, not simply through reproduction but also through the particularity of presence and relationship. This is the context for shalom. Man and woman needed each other, not in order to overcome or tame their bodies, but to delight in their Creator and in one another through their bodies. Here was the life they were called to live. This view of the creation of man and woman as dust and breath, in fellowship with each other and with God, stands at the core of a Christian conception of the body.

There is nothing in the biblical account of creation to hint that earthiness or human physicality is bad or problematic. Finite? Yes. All remain creatures and will never become the self-existent and self-sustaining Creator. That is and always remains reserved for God alone. Yet this finite creatureliness is not shameful or immoral but purposeful and good. The psalmist happily connects creation with God's wisdom:

> O Lord, how manifold are your works!
>> In wisdom you have made them all;
>> the earth is full of your creatures. (Ps 104:24)

Everything therefore still "looks to you" (Ps 104:27), the psalmist continues, since all remains dependent on the good and gracious Creator. Genesis and Psalms affirm our creatureliness and physicality as a great blessing, and our ongoing dependence on God as an even greater blessing. This is, you might say, "natural." Early Gnostics, not Christians, imagined the material body as part of an evil world created by a foul demiurge. Yet this antibiblical view of human origins has worked its way into the church and profoundly twisted the faith of many Christians. Irenaeus (d. 202) and other early Christian leaders consistently refuted such Gnostic corruptions; in the process they also unhesitatingly affirmed the goodness of creation, including our bodies.[8] To lose this affirmation was to risk losing the gospel, most especially the significance of the incarnate Son of God.

CONFUSION REGARDING EMBODIMENT

What are we to make of our bodies? On the one hand, Christian orthodoxy rejects the idea that we can reduce human existence to its material components. The human person is more than merely physical. Materialism claims that there is no soul or mind, so that if your body ceases, you (in all ways imaginable) no longer exist. Without getting into a technical philosophical debate, it is worth noting that the church has repeatedly rejected materialism as inadequate for handling the biblical data.[9] Human persons are not just a specific combination of oxygen, carbon, hydrogen, and the various elements that make up the human body.[10]

On the other hand, the recognition that we are more than material stuff should not cause us to devalue our bodies. Whatever *soul* and *body* designate, biblically and theologically they are intended to present a holistic portrait; here is a human person. The distinctive call of God is on humanity as he claims us, crafting us in his image (Gen 1:27; 5:2; Mal 2:15). Dutch theologian Herman Bavinck described what his contemporaries sometimes call the "dualistic holism" of the Bible:

> It is of the essence of humanity to be corporeal and sentient. Hence, man's body is first . . . formed from the dust of the earth and then the breath of life is breathed into him. He is called "Adam" after the ground from which he was formed. . . . The body is not a prison, but a marvelous piece of art from the hand of God Almighty, and just as constitutive for the essence of humanity as the soul (Job 10:8-12; Ps. 8; 139:13-17; Eccles. 12:2-7; Is 64:8). It is our earthly dwelling (2 Cor. 5:1), our organ or instrument of service, our apparatus (1 Cor. 12:18–26; 2 Cor. 4:7; 1 Thess. 4:4); and the "members" of the body are the weapons with which we fight in the cause of righteousness or unrighteousness (Rom. 6:13).[11]

It is unfortunately easy to treat the body and soul as two completely different parts of the human person, like two separable organs making up a compound creature.[12] This tends to pit the physical against the spiritual, with the result that one group of people will ignore or deny the existence of the soul and another will deny significance to the body.[13]

The Enlightenment, for example, tended to elevate the mind over physicality: it sought to control the body and through discipline to use it to accomplish goals while also questioning its intrinsic worth. Such a mindset viewed the body with deep suspicion. The body had very messy, earthy functions; it easily produced uncontrollable emotions or weakness, and thus it needed to be overcome. Enlightenment required independence of mind, which required independence of (and from) the body. It valued a consequent individualism and viewed dependence—both physical and relational—as weakness. The body was to be controlled for the purposes of physical health, performance, athletics, and so forth, so as to give our mental powers supremacy. The body existed solely for the mind.

More recently the "modern baroque" view of bodies, or what Elizabeth Hall labels as "the postmodern body," has taken hold in the West.[14] Modernity didn't deliver on its promises to produce peace, prosperity, and justice. We find ourselves instead in a fragmented society that has no agreed-upon norms. With the loss of a hope for justice and meaning, Hall argues, people turn to sensuality and self-indulgence, with bodily appetites demanding to be met while the consequences of indulgence are consistently underestimated or altogether ignored. Rugged individualism became radical individualism, so that self-absorbed "sensuality and pleasure has emerged as a reaction to modernity."[15] These responses still treat the body as something other than what it is; more like a marketable image to be observed than a life to be lived. In this way we can stand apart from our bodies as if we ourselves can watch and evaluate them. "Who are you" becomes a massively difficult question in today's swirl of image, projection, adaptation, modification, and suppression.

Recent developments in medical technology have enabled us to redefine ourselves physically according to the dictates of that ever-changing swirl. We have new tools to pursue whatever image today's popular ideal tells us we should look like. Botox delivers the changes, and Photoshop delivers the images. We can treat our bodies like blank canvases, with our imaginations and wallets as the only limits, redesigning and presenting them any way we prefer.[16] While this situation increasingly pushes us to objectify each other, studies further suggest that this consumerist conception of bodies has become so powerful that women—and increasingly men—often develop "self-objectification." This kind of objectification produces high levels of depression, shame, anxiety, sexual dysfunction, and eating disorders.[17] Like the experience of physical pain, this pursuit of a culturally dictated physical ideal often awakens our sense of not being in control.

When is it appropriate to use our improved medical technologies to change people's bodies? What if someone lacks the everyday physical functionality that others have? For example, how should we respond when someone is born with a cleft palette or Down syndrome? Or how does a man approach life when he loses a limb or gets Parkinson's disease? How should a woman respond when one day she can walk with ease and the next she is incapable of walking without help, even to her own bathroom? Physical functionality often waxes and wanes according to chronic pain conditions even in the course of a single day.[18] How do such complex bodily experiences affect our conception of our humanity? Whether we want to admit this theoretically, we do not separate our response to others, or our concepts of their identities, from their bodies. We are embodied, and we present ourselves to each other corporeally. Therefore, when our responses to people are informed more by marketing images than theological reflection, we see ourselves and others through distorting lenses and mistreat each other. We give undue preference to youth and strength, and we ignore those who do not fit the culture's ideals.

These questions form some of the tension that we live in today. On the one hand, we can be tempted to treat the body like it is something to be overcome and tamed through the power of our minds. On the other hand, the ways we express the value of our bodies are often destructive: we imagine that all our cravings should be met, or that we should conform to the currently reigning ideal of beauty and alter our physical shapes to match that. Each side, in its own way, misunderstands the body, compromises our identity, and produces a fragmented self. So how do we learn to see ourselves more holistically?

BONHOEFFER ON THE PURPOSE OF OUR BODIES

In 1933 Dietrich Bonhoeffer wrote a small but stimulating volume called *Creation and Fall* (*Schöpfung und Fall*). Some of his key observations about the purpose of embodied human creatures help us tie embodiment to relationality.

Bonhoeffer begins by drawing attention to how in the biblical narrative Yahweh fashions each aspect of the world, including humans. No abstract force pushes things forward. Genesis "expresses that it is really the Creator who makes me, the human being, with the Creator's own hands." Our bodily existence as shaped and brought forth by the Creator points to his "intention with me and nearness to me."[19] Raised from the earth, the human creature was made to commune with God. Genesis links humanity with the land, not as cursed but as good and fruitful. From the dirt comes the human person.[20] "It is God's earth out of which humankind is taken. From it human beings have their *bodies*. The body belongs to a person's essence."[21] Rather than viewing the body as some prison or empty shell for the human, Bonhoeffer affirms the integrity of our being in these two forms: "A human being is a human body. A human being does not 'have' a body—or 'have' a soul; instead a human being 'is' body and soul."[22] The Genesis account of creation celebrates the good unity of the human person, and it traces our connection to the earth—we really are what you might call "earthlings." Our existence occurs not as beings who drop out of the sky but rise from the dust. Filled with the divine breath, we live and then respond to his free love, entering into joyful communion with the Father who made all things.

Yet what about the human body is so peculiar, so meaningful? Bonhoeffer addresses that question by connecting our physicality to our relationality.

> In their bodily nature human beings are related to the earth and to other bodies; they are there for others and are dependent upon others. In their bodily existence human beings find their brothers and sisters and find the earth. As such creatures human beings of earth and spirit are "like" God, their Creator.[23]

Here Bonhoeffer draws from what is called the *analogia relationis* or the "analogy of relationship." Pointing back to the biblical description of the male and female created in the image and likeness of God (Gen 1:26-27), he argues that we are not like the triune God ontologically but rather relationally.[24] This relationality was always meant to include communion between the divine and human, between humans, and even between humankind and the rest of the earth.

Though we could rightly be called *spiritual* beings, this does not undermine our earthiness but rather hints at how we should understand it. Bonhoeffer argues that "in my whole being, in my creatureliness, I belong wholly to this world; it bears me, nurtures me, holds me."[25] Yet, as human creatures, we received the gift of freedom—freedom not to be the Creator, freedom not to be infinite, freedom not to be absorbed by another. It is actually a beautiful thing that the creature is not expected to be a god. And yet the wonder of this creaturely freedom is that we are not only to understand ourselves as free *from* the other but also as free *for* the other. This enables us to understand our distinctive call to exercise covenantal care over the rest of the earth. Bonhoeffer also believes that our creatureliness makes us interconnected beings, so that "without God, without their brothers and sisters, human beings lose the earth."[26] Our true freedom is freedom *for* others, and when we become isolated, we lose our way. It is not just our right relationship with God that is compromised when freedom is abused but also broken relationships with other people and even with the earth.

Our bodies, with all of their cumbersome finite limitations, call us back to this greater whole, to our place within creation and before the Creator. We have in common with animals "the same kind of body," that is, we both ultimately derive from the same dust and dirt. But while Adam could not find his fulfillment in them, he knew that he was not made to be alone. Although there were plenty of animals around, he needed someone who was *other* than but *like* him. God, in his grace, creates Eve from Adam's side, thus linking them together as distinctly human creatures (Gen 2:21-23). They belong to one another, even as they are distinguished from each other.[27] Adam can have no arrogance concerning this, for this embodied companionship was a gift. Isolation was never a good condition for the man or the woman.[28] Instead, God has created them to live in the freedom of fellowship with him and with each other, while also having set them free both *from* and *for* the creatures under dominion to serve them by ruling them. Therefore the qualities of faith, hope, and love have at their root a more communal rather than individualistic character.

Now Adam and Eve, the proper foundation for humanity, demonstrate the wonder of embodiment. According to Bonhoeffer, in this embodied human relationship they discover creaturely limits and the object of human love.[29] His observations deserve our attention:

> Knowing the other person as God's creature, simply as the other, as the other who stands beside me and constitutes a limit for me, and at the same time knowing that the other person is derived from me, from my life, and so loving the other and being loved by the other because the other is a piece of me—all that is for Adam the bodily representation of the limit that should make Adam's limit easier for Adam to bear. In other words, love for a person helps one to bear the limit.[30]

Brilliantly Bonhoeffer here connects love with human finitude. We are going to be, from the beginning, tempted to imagine we are gods, since we are such glorious creatures. We imagine ourselves as powerful, in control, and the masters of our own universe. Yet to encounter another, even in an unfallen world, is to encounter our finitude, our limits—never meant as a curse, yet always crucial to our happiness and life. We are embodied creatures, after all.

The *other* not only allows us to see our limits but also frames our love. "The other person is the limit that God sets for me, the limit that I love and that I will not transgress because of my love." Bringing the themes together, he declares, "By the creation of the other person freedom and creatureliness are bound together in love."[31] What Bonhoeffer prophetically understood was that when sin enters the world, it affects human relationships. And when relationships become fractured, the limits of the other person—which were good and could foster creaturely love and appreciation—often become objects of anger and frustration. When the love is lost, "a human being can only hate the limit. A person then desires only, in an unbounded way, to possess the other or to destroy the other."[32] Because we were made to worship God and live in the context of human community, this is devastating. The original grace of human companionship becomes a curse to us, for we see others as threats, as endlessly needy and demanding of us. Limits and love are interwoven in our bodily existence and consequent relationships.

Rather than functioning within the organic interconnectedness of God's good earth, fractured human people now view each other, and their own bodies, with irritation and even disgust. Our created bodily existence meant that from the beginning we needed the power of each other in order to live fully before God and enjoy his good world. When this joyful interdependence was compromised, shame, anger, and manipulation became the hallmarks of human relations. Now we are tempted either to dominate the other person's body or to run from their bodies because of the demands they may make of us. Yet each of these perversions points back to the original good. Our creaturely bodily existence was designed for life-giving human relationships that occurred under the benediction of God.

PHYSICALITY AND RELATIONSHIPS

Bonhoeffer's instincts, it seems to me, point us in the right direction. Though Elizabeth Hall doesn't interact with Bonhoeffer, her recent findings corroborate what Bonhoeffer intuited. Covering a vast terrain of psychology, sociology, philosophy, theology, and biblical studies, she shows again and again that our physicality appears to have real purpose, and that purpose relates to relationality. Even the social sciences now testify to the ways our bodies are "exquisitely geared to facilitate relationship."[33]

Psychologically the body orients us to the world and plays a crucial role in providing a script for us to live by. A mother's gentle caress of a newborn baby communicates to the child that she is safe and cared for. A warm hug from a friend gives a sense of belonging and comfort. A painfully sore back after a basketball game indicates that you might be a little too old to keep up with the young guys. Clearly, the intricate dynamics of our psychological relation to other persons hinge on the reality of our own embodiment.[34]

We also learn to relate with our bodies sociologically. You might say we learn the "rules of life" as we physically develop. A disapproving look from a parent informs an adolescent that their erratic behavior is out of line. An awkward dinner party reveals that you don't really know where to put your elbow. It doesn't take long to realize that the proper manner of our embodied existence depends to a significant degree on preestablished social norms.[35]

Kenneth Gergen's book *Relational Being: Beyond Self and Community* similarly critiques the Western conceptualization of self as a "bounded being."[36] In this tradition "selves" remain fundamentally separate—you begin where I end; my existence is not your existence. I contain me, and you contain you.

For Gergen the implications of this seemingly innocuous idea are staggering. A world of bounded being is a world of unrelenting evaluation, self-doubt, worship of the psyche, conditional love, self-gratification, self-celebratory monologues, and the society-wide pursuit of self-esteem. In such a world, "the number of ways in which we can fail is skyrocketing," and relationships may do little more "than remind us of some way in which we may be inadequate."[37] Proposing an alternative to this pale vision of humanity, and starting with decidedly religious words, Gergen writes, "In the beginning is the relationship." Gergen suggests all that is human is born of and sustained within relationship. I would add that this understanding of connection assumes and builds on the interconnectedness of our bodies, through which such relationships occur. Drawing on a variety of thinkers who have heavily informed sociologists, Gergen invites us to a new appreciation of self *with* others—the self as a "relational confluence."[38] What we must not miss is that this *self with others* assumes and affirms human bodies, but our distorted selves are easily tempted to think of others—with their bodily limits and psychological needs—as a burden to run from rather than as the way toward wholeness and hope. When we forget about the concrete earthiness of our relationships, which occur in and through bodies, then we do not simply lose *others* but, to use Gergen's language, we lose our very *selves*.

Philosophically, the body also plays an important role. The truth is that we do not have knowledge about the world apart from the mediation of our bodies. We relate ourselves to the world and learn about it through our eyes, ears, nose, hands, and feet. As Dallas Willard notes, "My perceptual consciousness is always marked by the specific state of my body. It is the same for every human being—that's part of our essence."[39] I cannot know right now what the underside of the desk I'm writing on looks like. Why? Because my head is above the desk looking at a computer on the top surface of the desk. My ability to perceive certain things is always dependent on the present state of my body.

Theologically, since our bodies are "for the Lord" (1 Cor 6:13), our bodies become significant means of displaying God's good intentions in his world— in other words, our bodies are public and point not merely to horizontal relations but also to vertical ones. Our bodies "are created by God to function in facilitating relationship, for the ultimate goal of showing God to others."[40]

We therefore cannot act as if we have complete control over our bodies or live as if our actions have no purpose beyond our own convenience and pleasure.

As the physical images of God on earth, we worship our Creator in a way that reflects and grows out of our creaturely humanity rather than in a way that denies or undermines it. Yet what are we to do when our pain threatens to undo us? What are we to make of the tyranny of suffering that can swallow even the most thoughtful and loving people, crushing them under its burdens? What are we to do when the falleness in the world distorts and deprives us of the good intended through our embodiment?

5

QUESTIONS THAT COME WITH PAIN

We must begin to proliferate the meanings of pain in order that we do not reduce human suffering to the dimensions of a mere physical problem for which, if we could only find the right pill, there is always a medical solution.

DAVID MORRIS, *THE CULTURE OF PAIN*

My flesh and my heart may fail,
but God is the strength of my heart and my portion forever.

PSALM 73:26

When I am sick I am not a mind with a suffering body, but I am the suffering body. Illness may then be the only time that we have the opportunity to discover that we are part of a story that we did not make up.

STANLEY HAUERWAS, *THE WOUNDED STORYTELLER*

Let us be unapologetic about our earthiness, about our physicality, since we know that the Creator Lord so made us and declared us good. Created for shalom as corporeal worshipers, we were called into communion with the King of creation and with fellow humans and even with the earth itself.

In contrast with that origin, not all is "good" or right with our physicality or with the relationships we are called into. The evidence lies everywhere: from the destructive tumors growing in our bodies to the dysfunctional relationships littering our lives. Our hearts oscillate between self-praise and self-condemnation, though neither is a stable or livable state. Between the chaos and the unanswerable questions, we sense the disconnect between our great need for spiritual life and the lack of any genuine experience of the deity's personal concern. In this struggle, there is little that awakens us to the brokenness of the world like physical pain and suffering. Sometimes that comes through our own bodies, but at other times it haunts us through the experiences of others. How are we, as Christians, to live in the midst of the pain?

Christians struggling with physical pain often develop defense mechanisms that are destructive in the long run. Denial, for example, can take many forms, like the cultivation of detachment from the pain. By deadening their affections and repressing their frustrations, some seek to carve out an inhabitable and safe space. Not only is this strategy only partially successful, but the colors of life soon dissolve into the blandness of grays and whites. While in some ways this path may allow a person to avoid becoming overwhelmed by the suffering, it normally also compromises relationships and flattens the complexity of existence that gives richness to life. Although the ones who close off the pain this way may not literally lie in the grave, those who know them whisper concerns about how "dead" they have become.

Justin, who had endured cancer and a series of deeply painful physical and emotional setbacks, explained to me how he ended up in a difficult place. He wrote,

> Growing up, I never talked about how I was truly feeling inside. So when I began to face hardships, I didn't know how to process them in a healthy way. I read God's Word and prayed, but I also began to depend upon other things that seemed to give me more immediate satisfaction, such as drinking heavily and abusing pills. Really, I sought after anything that would numb my physical and emotional pain.
>
> Eventually God gave me the gift of seeing and admitting my sin, and dealing with physical and emotional pain in healthy ways. I have learned that it is necessary to feel, and to be able to talk about those feelings with people and, most importantly, with God. He already knows our hearts and is there

to listen and forgive. Once I truly and honestly stepped down as CEO of my universe and found some rest in Him, He pointed me toward the one thing that will ultimately bring me comfort and hope: Himself.

Justin tried the common fix of denying the pain, deadening the emotions, and closing himself off. This led not to light but greater isolation and hurt, only adding to his genuine pain and struggle.

Others romanticize the pain. They link agony with extraordinary powers, astonishing spirituality, or an amazing triumph of the human spirit. Suffering Christians may sometimes be pressed by the urging of others to triumph over disease through "conquering unresolved sin." Unfortunately, many who try this response to pain discover neither unique mystical capabilities nor satisfying conquest. Instead, they discover that they do not necessarily become more spiritual or intimate with God. And while they have good days, too often they also have recurring nightmarish periods that speak not of the power of self-improvement but testify to their growing frailty, weakness, and dependence. These are the things the best-selling books don't tell you about. Those who start out with confidence on this path often end up exhausted on the sideline, struggling not to lose heart. What began sounding like profound encouragement can actually end up reverberating in the sufferer's ears like cruel, unrealized promises.

So is there another way? Is there a way to acknowledge the depth of the pain without falling into detached stoicism or naive triumphalism? The church has always believed that we do not testify properly to God if we lie about the state of the world. Sin, death, and devilish activity are all around us. Anguish, heartbreak, and troubled relationships are everywhere. *This* is the world we live in. And it is in this world that we must learn to live. Consequently, Christians are to live before God in this world by honestly facing the reality of pain's presence and all that it represents. We neither deny nor glorify it, but we must face it nevertheless, for this is the world we inhabit.

LEARNING TO LIVE IN THE PRESENCE OF DEATH

Mortality afflicts everyone, not just those who experience intense and prolonged suffering. Limiting the discussion to those who currently face intense suffering weakens our view of the problem, for all of us must learn to live in this pain-soaked world. None of us can predict what is around any corner.

And if we begin to see how this relates to us all, we might be in a better position to care for those who are intensely suffering and to understand why what the Gospels say is so amazing about Jesus—more on this in chapter six.

Throughout the history of the church, from the desert fathers to the Puritans, Christians have used the practice of meditating on death. That is partly because the question was not about the possibility of pain but how to live with it: prior to modernity the question was not "a choice between pain and sickness or relief, but between a willing and a reluctant endurance of pain and sickness," since all were constantly in some level of physical discomfort.[1] In medieval Christian art we often see a skull in the paintings of saints, representing their call to remember their mortality. Various Christian traditions that observe Ash Wednesday, which starts the Lenten season, also recognize the need to remember the fragile condition of our lives. The Book of Common Prayer, for example, gives these words as the ashes are imposed on the head of the believer: "Remember that you are dust, and to dust you shall return." This certainly can sound morbid to us, especially since, in our day, we do everything we can do to stay away from death, to isolate ourselves from the smells, sights, and sounds of human mortality. But it has long been considered an appropriate and even healthy reality to not just admit but even be mindful about the presence of death in our lives.

Countless Christians have heard or prayed the children's prayer, secured in their hearts through the New England Primer:

Now I lay me down to sleep,
I pray the Lord my soul to keep,
If I shall die before I wake,
I pray the Lord my soul to take. Amen.[2]

This nightly reminder brings the child (and parent!) to reflect both on the grace of life and its brevity, remembering that human life and health can be extremely fragile. And these words were memorized and prayed in premodern medicine days, when physical ailments were far too common for all in the household. Such mindfulness about our current compromised condition, it seems to me, is far from what is practiced by many of us today. Death, and all that leads up to it, is something we try not to speak of, much less meditate on. So why in classic Christian practices is there this apparent call to focus on such a morbid thought?

We creatures are necessarily fragile beings. We do others and ourselves no good by pretending this is not the case. Mutual dependence and engagement are integral aspects of created human experience and the context for joyful relationships. Even in light of the brokenness of our fallen world, we are still invited to be thankful for each day of life, recognizing that we cannot control or predict the future. We move into the future relying on God's faithfulness and love rather than on our current condition or prospects (Jas 4:13-16).

One important result of practicing an awareness of our mortality is that it can breed a greater concern for divinely given relationships. Historically, such heavenly mindedness was not meant to belittle this world but to value it, and to encourage the keeping of short accounts and always living in the present. You shouldn't hold a grudge or harbor hostility because you never know if you might die without making things right. When someone is aware of the brevity of life, each day can be received as a gift, offering opportunities and meaning not for some imaginary future but fully living in the moments that God has provided. Knowledge of death can also liberate people to live with courage in the present, even when it is risky: all die at some point, so be courageous and do the right thing since God will not let death be the final word. A sober awareness of a person's mortality can mean freedom from making self-preservation the highest value. In our day we often live somewhere between a fear of the past and the demanding possibilities of a mythical future. The untiring siren call of the future—with its grand plans to be accomplished, vacations to be had, retirements to be enjoyed—can become so strong it swallows our ability to live in the *now*. This often means people fail to be fully present, to live in the moment. We neglect spouses and children, disregard care for our bodies, and dismiss relationships that naturally require time and attention as an impossible luxury. We fall into this trap all the more easily when we are not mindful of our weakness and mortality.

Christians, who are regularly reminded that we are from dust and return to dust, also fall into this trap, but the gospel offers us a different perspective. Ironically, the practice of meditation on death does not freeze us in resignation but reminds us of the life we have in Christ. *You are alive*, so be present with God and neighbor. Confess your limits, and accept those of others; courageously move toward others that you might extend God's love to them, and they to you. This is the moment you have been given; this is the life you have been called to live. Don't worry about tomorrow, for tomorrow has more than enough worry on its own (Mt 6:34), and your anxiety cannot change the fact that we are not in control (Lk 12:22-34). Indeed, a proper appreciation of our mortality can clear our vision, enlightening us to the truly meaningful activities of this life.

When we are mindful of our mortality, we see the importance of keeping good relations with the Creator and his creation. Then, if we die unexpectedly, we are never unprepared to meet our Creator nor disheartened that we left dear ones without properly loving them. Keep short records; be mindful of our humanity, of our finitude, of our fragility. This goes against the reassurance of our achievements in the West, which tells us that we can always be growing stronger, more productive, higher, better. Such faith in achievement brings both the demand that we always improve ourselves and a sense of failure and rejection when success eludes us. When we are swept up in such "growth," we risk undermining our own humanity and devaluing the humanity of those around us, precisely because that philosophy is false and blinds us to reality. We can only be stretched so far before we break.

Between our present life and eventual death there remains some degree of space and time. Our present is not simply an uneventful string of motions but more like a sea that moves from beautiful calm to turbulent storm. In these various seasons of life we are called to exist in the present, not in denial of our mortality but mindful of it.

Because our culture teaches us not to expect suffering, when we face difficulties we panic, we grow angry, and we are ill equipped to deal with them. Our age of technological advance and medical achievement, along with the ways we isolate ourselves from sickness and death, has given us distorted expectations regarding our health. Older graveyards from centuries past contain too many little ones who died, too many young mothers, and too many of those who died were young. Horrific death was always either present or looming inescapably. Primitive medicine meant physical suffering was part of life in a fallen world. But now, even with the real limitations of modern medicine, we expect human bodies to function like machines: we should be able to run smoothly at all times. And if something goes wrong, just replace the part, shine us up, and then expect us to go back to peak performance.

Recharge battery, function perfectly, then recharge again. Rather than vocation and sabbath, we are machines with moments for recharge rather than genuine rest. We simply will not acknowledge our finitude.

We are not cell phones, automobiles checked against consumer reports for reliability, or devices on an assembly line. We are mortal human creatures. From birth we have great glory and goodness, but a darkness has made its way into our bodies and souls, a disharmony that lingers within us and throughout the earth. To the degree that we become aware of our physical, emotional, and spiritual dysfunctions, we mourn. While we each experience and respond to pain differently, it is (in our fallen world!) a universal phenomenon that none can deny.[3]

So how are we to live when our present moment includes a constant guest called pain? How are we to embrace the present moment, not just in light of the possibility of some future death but as we live in the midst of very real suffering? These questions are not easy. But learning to ask questions, to wrestle honestly with God amid our laments, can actually serve as a way to live faithfully before and with God in the present, even amid our struggle with pain.

JOB'S LAMENT AND OUR PAIN

David Kelsey, in his massive magisterial work exploring what it means to be human, argues that we should look not merely to Genesis 1–3 to frame our anthropology, but we should spend more time meditating on the biblical wisdom literature.[4] He is concerned not so much with what it means to be human in an ideal, pre-fallen world, which has an absence of sin and suffering. Instead, he wrestles more with how we should live in our present world, in the presence of sin and suffering. What is our present condition? In this spirit I would like to give a slow and careful reading of one chapter of the Bible's wisdom literature, Job 10.[5]

At this point in the book Job is struggling on several levels: his physical suffering is unrelenting, his friends keep delivering useless platitudes as advice, he has lost all his children and all his wealth, and he wrestles with God himself. The root of his pain is also the root of his faith, for Job knows that in the end all his frustrations and questions will end up at the feet of Yahweh. God is simultaneously Job's righteous Judge, who will set all things straight, and yet Job's Protector and Redeemer, who has allowed all that tragedy to enter his life.

Having suffered all the above-mentioned losses (Job 1–2), he pleads his case to God in Job 10, both lamenting and probing into God's intent. "I loathe my life," he says, speaking his complaint in "the bitterness of my soul" (Job 10:1). He uses his suffering as an investigative tool, concerned that God has condemned him when he doesn't understand why. What is it that God might have against him (v. 2)? Job's questions express the fear experienced by many who suffer, who often interpret their experiences as God's judgment and disapproval of them. Doesn't this pain and suffering somehow make it clear God is angry with me? Does God really dislike his people?

Knowing God is the just and ultimate Judge, Job recognizes that ultimately God alone can answer these hard questions. He asks whether the Maker of heaven and earth might also "despise the work of [his] hands" (v. 3). How could that be true of the good God who made all things well? But if God does not hate what he made, does he close his eyes and not see all the pain and anguish we all see? Is God blind? Job argues that his present suffering cannot be the result of any sin on his part, and God should know that (vv. 5-7). Perhaps it's the consequence of an earlier cosmic fall? Maybe, but he never mentions that here. He does seem confident that his current suffering cannot be understood as the result of his *personal* guilt. Consequently, this servant of God feels the tension between his belief in his Creator-Redeemer and his longing for deliverance: "Your hands fashioned and made me, and now you have destroyed me altogether" (v. 8). Job recognizes that he, like clay, started out as dust and will return to dust. Yet it is God who took this dust and fashioned from it a human creature, with "skin and flesh," with "bones and sinews" (v. 11). Has the Creator now abandoned his creation?

Job has not simply given in to despair, since he recognizes that grief has not been his only human experience. No, "you have granted me life and steadfast love, and your care has preserved my spirit" (v. 12). So how should he handle this tension and reconcile the presence of suffering and the promise of divine care? How can he hold together the goodness of the Creator and his awful, soul-gnawing, multidimensional aches? His answer is an appeal to divine mystery: "Yet these things you hid in your heart; I know that this was your purpose" (v. 13). We live in this tension. God will not give Job the kinds of answers that he seeks, even as Job is allowed to continue on with his speech. He understands that this holy Lord will not simply turn a blind eye to human sin, yet he sees no sin in him that would call for this grief and suffering. It is better, he imagines, not to try to understand, for it seems every time he lifts his head more waves of difficulty wash over him that seem to intensify his struggle (vv. 15-17). Given the unshakable presence of such suffering, wouldn't death be better than life (vv. 18-19)? Why—given the suffocating presence of pain during his short life—will God not just

> cease and leave me alone, that I may find a little cheer
> before I go . . .
> to the land of darkness and deep shadow,
> the land of gloom like thick darkness,
> and deep shadow without any order,
> where light is as thick darkness? (vv. 20-22)

Far too often we sound like Job's friends when we encounter those who suffer, whether from tragic events or physical pain. We start out strong, offering our sympathy and support. Job's friends sat silent with him for seven days and seven nights. They even lay there in the ashes with him, trying to show him "sympathy and comfort" (Job 2:11). Yet after the accepted time of mourning was over, they clearly had expectations of progress and resolve. After that accepted period, however, Job did not finally speak into the silence as a calm stoic. No, he spoke as a frustrated believer who laments his birth, which has now led to heartbreak rather than happiness (Job 3). He lives in pain:

> For the thing that I fear comes upon me,
>   and what I dread befalls me.
> I am not at ease, nor am I quiet;
>   I have no rest, but trouble comes. (Job 3:25-26)

With this break in the silence his friends begin to speak, even aware that their words may provoke his impatience (Job 4:1-2). But they speak, and so do we. As time moves on, we expect the wounded person to get better; we expect their frustrations and questions to turn into stoic acceptance. We expect denial or victory—ongoing struggle is the option we are most uncomfortable with, yet that is exactly where most who live with ongoing pain and suffering actually are.

Job struggles to make sense of his suffering in the context of his relationship with the Creator-Redeemer he worships. What are we to make of that struggle? First, we should note that Job's point of view fundamentally contradicts the many bad interpretations of the book that make it one of the most misused texts in the canon of Holy Scripture. It has been used to make God appear to be a capricious gambler or a tyrannical sovereign; Job has been misrepresented both as heroic antibeliever and as a sniveling weakling. Careful reading of the text shows far more complexity, richness, and theological depth than any flat reading can accommodate. It realistically examines human struggle in the context of persistent faith. It offers no simple answers, no easy formulas, but genuine wrestling and struggle.

For much of the history of interpreting the book, commentators have treated the beginning and end of Job as the really important parts. The opening introduces us to the Accuser, God, and a man named Job, who faces serial tragedies that befall him and those he loves (Job 1–2). And at the end we read that Yahweh finally addresses him, making it clear that Job is a created being rather than the one true Creator Lord (Job 38–42). Selections from these beginning and ending sections are normally the (only!) parts put into anthologies that include readings from this classic text. And yet, more recently, especially in our post-Auschwitz world, many have argued that the heart of Job is not the beginning and end, but the extended middle.[6] There we see debate, question, frustrations, ignorance, hope, and despair (Job 3–37). It can be easy to miss just how much of the book is devoted (thirty-four of forty-two chapters) to wrestling with God and others. What is so remarkable about this book is how God graciously allows so much space for the laments and struggles, not jumping in to swat Job down nor simply yelling from the heavens the right answers to all of his questions. God, it appears, is okay with giving us time to wrestle, not only with other people but even with God himself.

Near the end of the book we read, "Then the LORD answered Job out of the whirlwind" (Job 38:1). But what is the tone of God's voice; what is his attitude toward Job when he addresses him from the whirlwind? Our assumptions about that can determine our whole interpretation of the end of the book. We sometimes read it as if God is filled with anger, suppressing Job, humiliating him, and treating him with disdain.

There are good reasons, however, to read a very different tone of voice in Job 38. T. C. Ham, in a rigorously argued and scholarly informed essay, contends that "the tone of the YHWH speeches is closer to one of genuine compassion and comfort. . . . In speaking gently, God addresses Job's condition of suffering, without satisfactorily dealing with his concern over his innocence."[7] While I cannot repeat here his various linguistic and literary reasons for making these claims, I am persuaded his reading more faithfully represents the meaning of the text than does the assumption that God is mostly angry. Just a few comments will suffice. First, do not miss the stunning fact that the Creator God here condescends to a human, and even engages him in conversation.[8] In Yahweh's speech there is, of course, a clear contrast drawn between the wise and eternal Lord and the finite and struggling creature. God's power and wisdom are juxtaposed with Job's fragile situation. Yet while Job might have understandably feared that this God could crush him, instead Yahweh uses his superiority "to bring comfort to Job by introducing, reminding, and expanding Job's understanding of who precisely is speaking out of the whirlwind." As God speaks from the whirlwind, Job experiences "'the immediacy and directness of divine presence,' and not wrath."[9] Furthermore, the very giving of his name (YHWH), which only appears once between chapters 3 and 37, frames the discussion in terms of the covenant—this is the God who has made promises, who is present, and who is committed to his people. God's response to Job is a gentle and compassionate one, so that when he asks, "Who is this?," we should not read this as a "harsh reproof" but instead as a way that makes this conversation very personal and intimate.[10] We need not read God's call on Job to receive what he has to say "as a man" as negative; it can display the dignity of the Creator to his created image bearer, who should be able to receive these things from God. Again, we normally read God as chastising Job for his sins and ignorance, but the text actually consistently portrays God as declaring him "my servant" (Job 1:8; 2:3; 42:7-8 [4x]). Don't forget, at the end of this story God not only restores Job but gives him "twice as much as he had before," filling the rest of his days with blessing (Job 42:10-17). Even all of the rhetorical questions that follow in chapter 38 seem to "serve to soften God's tone, which would otherwise have seemed 'harsh, bragging, bullying' had the statements from God been phrased in the indicative." Instead, employing such an "interrogative form allows God to remind Job of divine wisdom and power 'with compassion and gentleness, albeit stern gentleness."[11] But do note that God's speech in Job 38 does not ultimately condemn or reject Job.[12] As Francis I. Anderson concludes, "There is no hint that God despises Job as unworthy of divine companionship; far from it. He invites Job to meet Him almost as an equal, standing up 'like a man' (Job 38:3)."[13]

What we discover in the book of Job in general, taking into account everything from his struggles in chapter 10 to God's response in chapter 38, is that God recognizes and fully understands Job's pain. It is a misreading of the text to imagine that God is belittling Job or the difficulty of his circumstances. That is far from the case. In the first century, James will encourage believers by pointing back to this biblical story, highlighting Job's faithfulness and God's concern: "You have heard of the steadfastness of Job, and you have seen the purpose of the Lord, how the Lord is compassionate and merciful" (Jas 5:11). Job is not disparaged, nor is God treated as insensitive or oppressive.

CONCLUSION

God's response to Job is not about his guilt or innocence; those issues and debates by Job and his friends are not actually answered by Yahweh. It may be that they all had misunderstood the true situation. But God often doesn't answer the questions we voice, even as he addresses the deeper concerns of our hearts. And as the readers of this sacred text our ultimate concern is not so much about why Job suffered, but why we do. Why do we have to live with the ongoing pain and frustrations? Yet, through the book of Job, we are taken to our deeper heart concerns. "A suffering person might exclaim, 'Why!' but the answer is rarely 'Because,' but 'Here I am.' . . . In the book of Job, it is YHWH who answers, 'Here I am.'"[14]

Job's suffering and God's response paint a compelling picture for Christians who suffer today. Our pain may seem to overshadow the light of God's presence, but in the honest cries of our lament and grief we may, like Job, hear something beyond the answer to our questions. We might hear and know the presence of the God who not only is here but who has borne for us the weight of all that is broken, who absorbed not only our sin but also the chaos of disease and death in all its forms. It is in our cries that we can learn that *this God comes.*

God, addressing ancient Israel through the book of Job, declares, "You don't understand, and yet you do understand. I have not yet revealed how I will overcome this problem of pain and suffering, how I will fix my compromised creation." God will redeem it, but not like anyone expected.

God answers Job, ultimately, not by lecturing him (as we often understand the conclusion of Job); no, God will ultimately answer Job's questions by *becoming* Job's substitute. God will enter the human predicament. He who is Spirit will take on flesh and become fully human. He will not only see physical pain everywhere but experience it deeply himself, and he will defeat sin and all the chaos it brings about, both in the human heart and in all our relationships. The Son of God comes as God's great answer to Job's deepest questions and concerns. He comes silently, quietly, humbly. *But he comes.*

PART II

THE STRANGENESS OF GOD

6

ONE WITH US

INCARNATION

Jesus wept,
And in his weeping,
he joined himself forever
to those who mourn.
He stands now throughout all time,
this Jesus weeping,
with his arms about the weeping ones:
"Blessed are those who mourn,
for they shall be comforted."
He stands with the mourners,
For his name is God-with-us.
Jesus wept.

ANN WEEMS, *PSALMS OF LAMENT*

For in [Christ] the whole fullness of deity dwells bodily.

COLOSSIANS 2:9

He sanctified the body by being in it.

ATHANASIUS, *ON THE INCARNATION*

So what is God's response to Job and to us regarding the chaos, sin, and suffering of this world? Thus far in this book it is as if I have plotted points on a graph: questions about whether God cares, concerns about responding to the problem of pain, the reality of our longing mixed with lament, and making sense of how our bodies relate to both the original and compromised creation. It is time now to connect the dots. When a line is properly drawn between these points, what we find staring back at us is a human face, the face of Jesus the Messiah. And when we finally look into the eyes staring back at us, the entire question of our suffering looks and feels different, from our longings and our laments to our nagging hard thoughts about God and our frustrations with the pain we cannot defeat.

God's response to this chaos and sin and suffering is that *God takes responsibility*! God himself comes forward to deal with the mess. "God stands in solidarity with the world," John Swinton observes, "and [he] takes responsibility for the evil and suffering in this world."[1] As Swinton notes, this does not mean that God is to blame for our condition. God concerns himself for us in our sin and pain, neither because it was required of him nor because he had personally done anything wrong, but because he loves us and is the only one who could restore what was lost, repay the debt, free the slave, and heal the sick. He alone could save us from the mess we had made of ourselves.

The way that God takes responsibility for our condition is by becoming one of us. The Son's incarnation, suffering unto death, and bodily resurrection are God's answer. In these three movements, God takes possession of our sin, misery, and battle with suffering. This reality refutes any conception of a distant and unconcerned deity, for God enters our world to handle this cosmic crisis.

Jesus was a particular human being, a first-century, Palestinian, Jewish man. In his humanity he was like us in all ways. He is God's solution. John the apostle marveled at this earthy fact, beginning his first epistle by describing his sensory experiences of being with this person.

> That which was from the beginning, which we have *heard*, which we have *seen* with our eyes, which we *looked* upon and have *touched* with our hands, concerning the word of life—that life was *made manifest*, and we have *seen* it, and *testify* to it and proclaim to you the eternal life, which was with the Father and was *made manifest to us*. (1 Jn 1:1-2, my emphasis)

What was made manifest? Jesus was no ghost, no phantom. His body was no magical illusion. This man, born in Bethlehem and brought up in Nazareth, was the incarnate Son of God. As strange or wonderful as this may sound to us, it sounded even stranger to first-century Jewish ears. John adds, "That which we have seen and heard we proclaim also to you, so that you too may have fellowship with us; and indeed our fellowship is with the Father and with his Son Jesus Christ" (1 Jn 1:3). Not only was Jesus God *with* us, but he was also God *for* us. John understood that this fleshly Jesus was the pathway to renewed relations with the Creator himself. Jesus reestablished our fellowship with the triune God. Out of the Father's love the Son and Spirit are sent to carry out the work of re-creation in our lives and this world. To embrace Jesus, the embodiment of God's mind-bending condescension, is to trust in the loving provision of the triune God (cf. 1 Jn 4:1-3). Here is the invitation. To look to the Son and love him is to enter into the life-giving fellowship of the Father, Son, and Spirit. For John, this spiritual truth is understood in very concrete terms: hear, see, touch. The physicality of the Messiah takes us to the heart of the gospel and God's promise, not just of sympathy but of rescue. God has come, come near, come to be God with us and God for us!

Tonya is only in her thirties and yet has already been through far more difficulties than most of us care to imagine. Listening briefly to her story can help us begin to appreciate why the incarnation matters to believers on a most practical and personal level. These are her words:

> God has taught me what it means to have dependence on him not only for salvation but for the pain of this present life. He did not teach me this dependence through the ministry of my church or family (I am a pastor's kid and a pastor's wife); he taught me dependence through my personal experiences of suffering.
>
> During my freshman year of college, my dad was diagnosed with cancer. He battled bravely for four years, but died during my senior year. Several years later, my husband and I welcomed our third child. Three days after he was born, I was diagnosed with breast cancer and began two years of treatments and surgeries. A few months later, I became pregnant with our fourth child, but had a miscarriage, which led to a complete hysterectomy.
>
> Feelings of pain and loss soon spiraled out of control, and I fell into a deep depression. To cope, I began to abuse prescription medication as well as alcohol.

Occasional abuse quickly became an enslaving addiction, and I spent the next fourteen months in a residential addiction treatment program.

Amid some of my greatest times of pain and being alone, I was reminded and comforted by the fact that Jesus Christ understands physical pain. There was one day, in particular, in treatment when I was feeling the loss of my family, I was feeling physical pain, and I was feeling misunderstood and hopeless. God brought his word to my heart. He caused me to meditate on his name Emmanuel, which means "God with us." I felt his presence in a way I hadn't before. God, in his incarnation, was with us. He knowingly came to earth and suffered not only physical pain but emotional pain. He felt the pain of abandonment in the garden when crying out to his father.

When I would lie in bed after surgeries, or when I was alone in treatment, I would be reminded that God "gets it." All he wanted from me was honesty. I could tell him how I felt, even if it was that I was angry and frustrated, and I knew he truly understood. How awesome that I can worship a God who understands pain and will hear me and comfort me even in, especially in, my rawest emotions. Not only was God "with us" through his incarnation but even now he is "with us" through the Holy Spirit.

Living through wave after wave of grief, physical pain, disappointment, and frustrations, Tonya found profound comfort by meditating on the fact that the Son of God took on real flesh and blood, becoming one with us. And in some powerful ways, this also opened up for her a richer confidence that she was a child of God, loved by the Father, understood by the Son, and kept by the Spirit. By meditating on Christ, she found herself ever more confident that she was in God's family, which brought profound comfort and courage to her in trying times.

Many of the early church fathers understood this invitation into life-giving fellowship with God through the Pauline notion of adoption (2 Cor 6:18; Rom 8:15-17). For these church fathers the entire purpose of Jesus' condescension was to reestablish the familial bond between God and humanity that had been broken by the fall. Although Jesus is the only one who will ever possess the quality of eternal sonship with the Father (Son by nature), his redemptive work transforms believers into daughters and sons of God by grace (by adoption).[2] Ultimately, this is the end goal of Jesus' earthy existence. Theologian Donald Fairbairn captures this idea well when he concludes, "The incarnation was the movement of God that made it possible for human beings who had lost their relationship with God to be restored to that fellowship again . . . because humanity lost that fellowship through the Fall, God the Son personally stepped into human existence in order to make us his adopted brothers and sisters."[3]

To further appreciate the profundity and beauty of Jesus' incarnation, let us begin by traveling back almost two millennia to a turbulent time in the ancient church; here we meet one emerging Christian leader in particular who was trying to understand why Jesus was so important. His answer might help us begin to think differently of Jesus, our bodies, and even our pain.

WHY THE CREATOR COMES—ATHANASIUS

Near the beginning of the fourth century a young man—from the age of five to eleven—lived during the persecutions in Egypt, which ended in 311. In his early years he not only received a Greek education but also spent time at some point in the Egyptian desert learning from the life of St. Anthony.[4] Though his writings would eventually become a pillar of Christian orthodoxy, he wrote probably his most important work *before* he was even twenty and prior to having any proper title or position. His name was Athanasius, and the early book was titled *On the Incarnation of the Word of God* (*De Incarnatione*). While Athanasius will forever be remembered for his willingness to defend the faith amid great challenges during the later Arian controversies, it was this early treatise that first demonstrated his profound ability to capture the heart of the Christian faith. In that work Athanasius helps us begin to grasp the significance of what the incarnation tells us about God and his relationship to his creation.

Athanasius ponders this fundamental question: Why would the Word of God, in his grandeur and greatness, become "manifest in bodily form" and as such, become truly human?[5] His answer is that the incarnation occurs both out of the Father's great love and for the purpose of our "salvation." Yet, rather than imagining salvation as something abstractly spiritual, Athanasius described this salvation as inherently earthy.[6] It is about the "renewal of creation," and such cosmic *re*-creation is appropriate only for "the Self-same Word Who made it in the beginning."[7] Here Athanasius shows an awareness of our temptation to pit heaven against earth, spirituality against physicality, Old against New Testament. But this is to make enemies of what should be friends. "There is no inconsistency between creation and salvation; for the One Father has employed the same Agent for both works."[8]

Here are the questions Athanasius raises: What were God's options in light of the original rebellion that brought chaos and human death into the world (cf. Gen 2:16-17; 3:1-24)? Might the righteous Lord of creation decide that fallen humanity deserved pain and death as their new solidified reality? Given his strong view of the goodness of the original creation, Athanasius believes that if we are not careful about how we try to answer these questions, we will end with a misunderstanding of the Maker of all things. If God simply decided to abandon fallen humanity, or even just destroy us immediately, this would raise all kinds of concerns. It may be that *logically* God could have opted for such a response, but Athanasius thinks such options would have been deeply problematic. No, it would be "monstrous and unfitting" for God to ignore or utterly destroy his creation, for this would appear more like the victory of the devil rather than the justice of God.[9]

But God's good world was now headed toward utter destruction, so "what then was God, being good, to do? Was he to let corruption and death have their way with them?" According to Athanasius, "Such indifference to the ruin of His own work before His very eyes would argue not goodness in God but limitation, and that far more than if He had never created men at all." In light of the goodness of God's original creation of humanity, Athanasius somewhat controversially concludes, "It was impossible, therefore, that God should leave man to be carried off by corruption, because it would be unfitting and unworthy of Himself."[10] Leave humanity in their sin and pain? It just wasn't an option, according to Athanasius.

God can't ignore his creation, but neither can he "falsify Himself," acting like no wrong had occurred.[11] Sin had already produced cosmic shock waves; the entire creation was now infected and affected by sin—death was woven into the fabric of all human existence. Only Life itself could overcome the new dominion established by death and the devil. But Life cannot work if it stands aloof, for it must enter into the territory of death; it must find and heal what had led to death itself. Put differently, Athanasius believes *this battle and our salvation necessarily take place in and through human bodies.*[12]

Despite all our talk of the spirituality of Christ's work, Athanasius understands this spiritual battle in physical terms: "The Saviour assumed a body for Himself, in order that the body, being interwoven as it were with life, should no longer remain a mortal thing. . . . He put on a body, so that in the body He might find death and blot it out."[13] Since sin had occurred in and through the body, it now affects us physically in subtle and profound ways. Consequently, sin must now be overcome *in the body*. Thus, the Creator Lord, in order to defeat sin, must enter the brokenness by taking to himself a genuine human nature, which includes a real body. Only through this particularity, through the condescension of the Holy One, can a cosmic reversal begin. It must begin in his body before it can then affect all of our bodies.

Just to show that Athanasius is not alone in this kind of thinking, notice that Augustine, sometimes called the father of orthodoxy, employs similar logic. In light of how sin has affected the earth, including human bodies, God considers various ways to heal humankind. Working backward from the evidence, Augustine concludes, "He found no better way" to give us "benefits" and meet our "interests" than by the incarnation, that is, "taking to himself the *whole* man."[14] He insists that this must be real incarnation, a real humbling for the eternal Son of God as he assumes a human nature. The Son could not merely look human but must become a "real human being to human beings." Why? Because "the same nature had to be taken on as needed to be set free." It is worth adding that Augustine also recognizes that part of our humanity, and thus part of Jesus', is our sexuality. Knowing that for him to be a concrete human being, to embrace bodily limits and particularity, this would also mean that Jesus would need to represent male and female, *but* he could not be both male and female at the same time. That would undermine his genuine embodiment, his genuine humanity. Particularity is part of creaturely life. Thus, this is why "lest either sex should imagine it was being ignored by the creator, he took to himself a male and was born of a female."[15] In this way Augustine saw the incarnation as representing us all without compromising the concrete particularity of the humanity of Christ. Thus his temptations, and even his pain and suffering, would all maintain both a particularity and universality to them. As the new Adam he would be able to represent the whole without ceasing to be a particular person (cf. Rom 5:12-21).

Returning to Athanasius, let us not miss the organic way that he appears to tie all of humanity together. While this ancient preacher never doubted the reality that all of us sin and are sinners, he was not trying to make direct correlations between one's personal pain and God's judgment against an individual for his or her particular iniquities. Remember Job? This was the problem with his friends' speeches: they imagined direct cause and effect could be established between sin and affliction, but God lets them know that they were wrong. While the servant Job may have been faithful and even free from personal guilt on particular matters raised against him (Job 1:1, 8; 2:3; 42:7-8), he nevertheless remained, like all of us, within this cosmic web of distortion and brokenness. Athanasius tries to remind us that human physical suffering and misery are part of a much larger problem, going back to Genesis 3. In other words, whether we feel a gnawing ache in our bones or a penetrating throbbing in our heads, this points to a cosmic problem. But such physical agony doesn't *neces-sarily* point directly to anything we have done to deserve this suffering.

According to Athanasius, the incarnation became necessary in the sense that only such a move could address the entrance of sin into God's good world. Human sin created a kind of cry that rose to the heavens and was received like a call to the loving Creator such that God "made haste to help us and to appear among us."[16]

God's answer to our cry was not a *what*, notes Athanasius, but a *Who*. "For He alone, being Word of the Father and above all, was . . . able to recreate all, and worthy to suffer on behalf of all."[17] He took "a human body even as our own," one that was genuinely physical and "liable to the corruption of death."[18] Ultimately, according to Athanasius, it required the sacrifice of Jesus' own body—so that he personally faced death—for death to be overcome. This death and the following resurrection victory serve as a shockwave that moves out from Jerusalem and slowly awakens the world to a new beginning. We will speak more on these points in the next two chapters.

Athanasius understood that our theology cannot simply jump to the death of Jesus but must first appreciate the significance of the birth and life of this unique Messiah.[19] He understood that this battle was a physical one, and it needed to take place in the flesh, even the flesh of Christ. The cure of sin required that the Garden of Eden be revisited; only this time the "last Adam" (*eschatos adam* [1 Cor 15:45]) would prove faithful where the first Adam failed.[20] This Adam would bring life to the human experience where death had been reigning.

Finally, Athanasius ties the incarnation to revelation. He argues that when the Son comes, he comes not only to enter into solidarity with us for the purpose of redemption but also to give us a restored picture of the Father in his love and grace.[21] Since sin affected us holistically, it not only corrupted our bodies, bringing physical pain and death, but it also corrupted our vision of God himself. Fallen humanity was left to imagine God as cruel and unconcerned. This again gets to the hard thoughts about God we might be tempted to have. Jesus, the Word of God incarnate, replaces the distorted picture of God that we have with an accurate portrait of the Father of the Lord Jesus Christ. God's holy and paternal love is beautifully *re*-presented in the coming of the Son.[22] We have a chance, through the incarnation, to have a restored vision of the God who is, rather than a distorted image of a god we fear. This renewed knowledge "of their Maker is for men the only really happy and blessed life."[23] Put simply, to see Jesus is to see the Father, for he comes from the Father and reveals the Father full of grace and truth (Jn 10:25-38).

JESUS' EMOTIONS AND HUMAN SUFFERING—WARFIELD

"It belongs to the truth of our Lord's humanity, that he was subject to all sinless human emotions." These words come near the beginning of B. B. Warfield's essay titled "On the Emotional Life of our Lord," published in 1912.[24]

One of the great and surprising challenges for Christians is truly affirming Jesus' full humanity. And yet, according to the early Christian creeds, acknowledging the complete humanity of Jesus is just as vital to Christian belief as recognizing his true divinity.[25] As a way to test our claims about Jesus' authentic humanity—and his solidarity with us—we can examine how we tend to view his "emotional life," if we consider it at all. Since so much of what we learn about his emotions in the Gospels comes in the context of physical suffering and death, these reflections are of great relevance to our particular study. Truly, Jesus' emotions call us to revisit the land of lament and longing, as well as promise and hope.

Warfield might be viewed as an odd choice of writers for examining Jesus' emotions and their relationship to physical suffering. Spanning the nineteenth and twentieth centuries (1851–1921), this Princeton theologian is often stereotyped as "rationalistic," which is rarely meant as a compliment. He was raised and educated in the fading tide of the Enlightenment, a movement whose impulse was to elevate objective rationality and devalue subjective emotions. Those familiar with Warfield's name are quick to compare him to a scientist but slow to think of him as a poet exploring the inner life of humans. And yet in Warfield's personal life we see deep emotional pain, sacrifice, and affectionate love. In the end, his own experience, despite his rationalist leanings, made him keenly able to write such an insightful piece of biblical exposition.

When he was twenty-five years old, Warfield married Annie Pearce Kinkead.[26] Shortly after their wedding they traveled to Europe, where Warfield extended his studies under leading German scholars of the day. During their time overseas, this young couple was walking in the Harz Mountains in Germany when a violent thunderstorm caught them unawares. Annie suffered some sort of nervous breakdown from which she would never recover. Indeed, she spent the rest of her life as a kind of invalid. For the next thirty-nine years Warfield traveled little as he organized his schedule and work so as to be her primary caregiver. The couple never had children, and it is reported that Warfield would not be away from Annie for more than an hour or two at a time. Even as he cared for his frail wife, Warfield simultaneously built a career as an internationally recognized scholar. Although it is unclear exactly what originally happened to Annie that caused her difficulties that remained with her for the rest of her life, what is clear is that Warfield experienced daily reminders of the fallenness of the world, the reality of pain, the nuance of tenderness, and the power of concrete love expressed in action. Such experience may have been exactly what put Warfield in a position to explore with uncanny insight the emotional life of Jesus his Lord. For him redemption only made sense in light of Jesus, the Son incarnate, because the truly human Jesus, with his emotions, points us to the heart of God.[27]

Warfield saw in the Gospels a portrait of the Messiah that included a wide variety of emotions. According to Warfield—and more recent scholarship has only reinforced this claim—compassion is the emotion most often attributed to Jesus in the biblical narrative.[28] Jesus "was moved with compassion" again and again (e.g., Mt 9:36; 14:14; 15:32; 20:34; Mk 1:41; 6:34; Lk 7:13), and this meant a kind of "internal movement of pity," which occurred when appeals to his mercy were made. Jesus' compassion inevitably led to action.[29] Rather than seeking emotional detachment, when Jesus sees the blind men (Mt 20:34), a bereaved widow (Lk 7:13), or the leper in need of cleansing (Mk 1:41), his response is consistently a "heart throbbing with pity," which is moved to action. Further, this compassion is directed toward people who experience some form of bodily pain or suffering. That may be hunger, disease, or physical isolation fostered by social and religious judgment. Jesus embodied compassion, felt it, and expressed it toward those in the grip of agony and sorrow.

Behind this power of compassion was Jesus' wholehearted love toward those around him. Warfield notes that the Messiah's "prime characteristic was love, and love is the foundation of compassion."[30] Jesus lives in love for his Father and a love for sinful humanity. This compelling love informed his whole life's mission, so that Jesus serves as the embodiment of the two greatest commandments. Self-giving love is a hallmark of Christian discipleship today because it was determinative in the life of the Savior. And imitating this Jesus, especially his cross—which we will talk about next chapter—becomes the pattern for how Christians understand living amid those who suffer. Although Jesus' life does give us a pattern to imitate, it is his own life as a life of love that lives within us (Gal 2:20). For now let us notice that his deep love pushes Jesus forward, stirred on by "the joy that was set before him" (Heb 12:2), which includes the promise of new life, healing, and hope for his people who will be under his loving reign and rule yet again.

Among other emotions Warfield discusses, his exploration of anger in the life of Jesus is the most stimulating. While many shy away from attributing anger to Jesus, Warfield notes that truly righteous people cannot maintain their character if they look upon evil and injustice while remaining indifferent. Jesus rightly grows angry when onlookers display amazingly hard hearts; they appear to care more about whether Jesus might break a regulation by healing on the sabbath than about a man suffering from a withered hand (Mk 3:5). Elsewhere Jesus demonstrates a milder form of anger, which Warfield considers "annoyance" or "irritation," as displayed when his disciples keep children from him (Mk 10:14). Yet Warfield's exposition of Jesus at the tomb of Lazarus is most insightful in this regard, and it bears the greatest relevance for our understanding of our own physical pain.

Warfield draws attention to the fact that Jesus, as he stands before the grave of his beloved friend surrounded by the grief of others, is twice described as "groaning in his spirit" (Jn 11:33, 38). In fact, the word (*enebrimēsato*) is better translated as *rage*: "the emotion which tore his breast and clamored for uttermost was just rage."[31] Jesus was not angry with Mary or at others present. As he faced the sights, sounds, and smells of grief and death—the culmination of physical suffering—he was angry at the destruction caused in the world by the entrance of evil. Jesus' tears grow out of this rage, and he weeps (Jn 11:35). In this scene it is "brought poignantly home to his consciousness the evil of death, its unnaturalness, and its 'violent tyranny.'" John's Gospel, in this episode, makes it clear that Jesus came "not in cold unconcern, but in flaming wrath against the foe."[32] The agony, the tyranny, the domain of suffering and death was just too much. As Athanasius wrote, "Man . . . was disappearing, and the work of God was being undone."[33] This situation cannot stand. Jesus declares himself "the resurrection and the life" even before his own death and rising (Jn 11:25) and gives everyone there a small taste of a future reality. Before their eyes he demonstrates his power over death. He says, "Lazarus, come out. . . . Unbind him, and let him go" (Jn 11:43-44)—and it is done.

Jesus of Nazareth was no stoic. His life demonstrates a richness of emotions, including painful emotions that are inescapable when a person lives in a fallen world. Against the backdrop of personal pain and sacrifice, B. B. Warfield was able to examine and clarify this rich emotional life of Jesus, showing his profound compassion for the wounded and his deep anger at the way pain and death constantly dominated humanity. Resolution *must* come.

CONCLUSION

Athanasius and Warfield both understood, in their own ways, how important the life of Jesus was for understanding the ways of God. Jesus' incarnational existence, including his emotions and pains, points us back to the gracious and holy Creator. Jesus also points us forward to new hope, to new life. God achieves the new in us not by obliterating the old but by entering our situation, taking it for his own, and then transforming it. Sent in both the Father's love and in the life-giving power of the Spirit, the Son's incarnation, his taking on true and full human nature, means that our Savior understands us in the most intimate and reassuring ways. The Son of God has taken on flesh, has felt physical pain, and has even entered the unutterable darkness of death itself. Jesus, Emmanuel, becomes the great sympathetic high priest who understands our fears, our pain, our temptations, our weaknesses (Heb 4:14-16) by making them his own. But Jesus will be more than merely sympathetic. The incarnate Son comes from the Father and in the Spirit, not merely to appreciate human suffering but to overcome it. The Creator has called to his creation, and the Word who first called the creation into existence has now entered the world of flesh and blood. He has come. The only thing that could possibly be more stunning than the fact that he comes is the discovery that he comes to die. This is no mere mission of investigation but rather of rescue and redemption. Therefore it is now time to face the darkness of the cross, but also to prepare for the sunrise of resurrection.

7

ONE FOR US

CROSS

Only the suffering God can help.

Dietrich Bonhoeffer, *Letters and Papers from Prison*

When the thief beheld the author of life hanging upon the cross, he said: "If it were not God made flesh that is crucified with us, the sun would not have hid its rays nor would the earth have quaked and trembled."

Lenten Triodion

He himself bore our sins in his body on the tree, that we might die to sin and live to righteousness. By his wounds you have been healed.

1 Peter 2:24

While sitting around a table with a group of pastors talking about suffering and faith, I was struck by our difficulty in making sense of it. All bore the scars of countless bedside conversations and numerous sleepless nights in which they wrestled with God in prayer and cried with those they loved. We were at our best as we shared stories of these experiences, stories of courageous fathers facing certain death and yet praising God, tales of godly women who

received misdiagnoses and yet endured awful pain without growing bitter. All of these were true. All of these were helpful stories.

Finally an unavoidable question surfaced and lingered, though we all were a bit self-conscious voicing it: *Why do our physical sufferings really matter?* The Scriptures so often link suffering and affliction to persecution (e.g., Jas 1:2-3; 2 Cor 1:8-9; 11:23-27) that Christians may wonder whether this is the only kind of suffering God counts as meaningful or worth consideration.

JESUS' DEATH REQUIRES AN INCARNATE LIFE

One of the challenges we face when handling Scripture is that we can pay so much attention to single verses that we end up with an atomized reading of the Bible, thus compromising the power of the larger story Scripture draws us into. It can be easy to lose a vision of the whole when so much focused attention is given to the parts. Along these lines, it is easier than we realize to lose sight of the *reality* of incarnation as we deal with the swirl of specifics in Scripture. Especially for those of us who focus on the significance of Christ's death, the earlier radical act in which the eternal Son assumed a particular human nature can become neglected in the story of redemption, as if one could ever understand the cross apart from the body of Jesus! Consequently, we often undervalue the fact that the Son took to himself a genuine body capable of experiencing pain—it is *his* body, and thus this is nothing short of *him*. Simply put, there is most certainly no Christian gospel apart from the Son becoming a single embodied human being.

At least two factors incline us to neglect the significance of Christ's life in a physical body. First, sometimes because the church worries that the world doesn't account for spiritual realities, Christians can compensate by undervaluing the physical and overemphasizing *spiritual* concerns. All of a sudden the only thing that matters to some Christians is what is "spiritual"; when that happens we are tempted to neglect the importance of physicality. Second, we Westerners so emphasize a merely legal understanding of the death of Christ for our salvation that we overlook material in the New Testament that doesn't fit that model. Instead, Christians should also use the material that occurs before Passion Week in the Gospels to understand the salvation that Jesus has brought us. Specifically, the Son took to himself a human body capable of experiencing all the pain and suffering that we do, and this physicality was the context of his teachings, his words, and his actions.

I sometimes even hear Christians downplay the physicality of Jesus' death while emphasizing his "spiritual suffering." Some of this may have its roots in early Protestant attempts to distance themselves from a Roman Catholic overemphasis of his physical pain at the crucifixion.[1] These days it may also result from modern squeamishness at the brutality of crucifixion. In any case, since Christianity insists on the full deity and the full humanity of Christ, we have to attend the physical as well as the spiritual side of Jesus' life and death. Dividing the spiritual from the physical can only distort our understanding of the gospel, of Jesus, and of ourselves. The biblical story is necessarily a physical one, as well as spiritual, from start to finish. And this takes us to the most shocking revelations found in the Bible.

God, who cannot get sick, who cannot grow hungry, who cannot bleed, who cannot die—*this* God comes near so that the impossible becomes possible. As Athanasius realized, "It was precisely *in order to be able to die* that He had taken a body."[2] But he does not just die, *he comes to live!* Solidarity, representation, and hope suddenly materialize in unexpected and even disturbing ways as the truth of Jesus' full identity emerges—in this way he is both "with us" and "for us."

HIS DEATH IS THE CULMINATION
OF HIS IDENTIFICATION WITH US

The Son of God does not fall from heaven as a thirty-year-old man hanging on a cross. No one really thinks this, but we often approach the gospel as if we did. The Gnostics, not the Christians, longed to be removed from the material world that might defile neatly packaged spiritual ideas with physical messiness. How upset they must have been to hear that the One, the Creator of all, took on sticky human flesh and lived for nine months in the womb of the Virgin Mary. Jesus lived a flesh-and-blood-and-bone life in a messy, complex, and fallen world. Luke explains, "Jesus increased in wisdom and in stature and in favor with God and man" (Lk 2:52; cf. 1 Sam 2:26), indicating gradual human experience that includes genuine development. The purpose of the incarnation was not that Jesus merely dies but that he lives as one *with* us, and only then to offer himself as one *for* us.

The Son's assumption of a human nature produces solidarity between Creator and creature: Jesus becomes the one mediator between God and humanity (1 Tim 2:5).[3] Sent from the Father and in the power of the Spirit, the Son enters the human experience as a particular, concrete Jewish man who comes with the purpose of healing. "For he who sanctifies and those who are sanctified all have one origin. That is why he is not ashamed to call them brothers and sisters" (Heb 2:11).[4] Our sanctification—our being made holy—rests upon the Son's incarnation. When the Son "put on our flesh," John Calvin observes, "the author of holiness and we are made partakers" of this shared humanity—we have "one origin."[5] Because of this connection, nothing less than "the body of Jesus Christ" serves as the means through which our sanctification occurs (Heb 10:10). God, the one "for whom and by whom all things exist," promises to bring many to glory in a "fitting" manner: he accomplished this by making "the founder of their salvation perfect through suffering" (Heb 2:10), possible only because the Son took to himself a physical body. The Son fuses himself with our pain, our weakness, our fears, our struggles. To rescue fallen humanity, none other than God himself comes as one of us, among us, for us. Karl Barth expresses this point thus:

> The Almighty exists and acts and speaks here in the form of One who is weak and impotent, the eternal as One who is temporal and perishing, the Most High in the deepest humility. The holy One stands in the place and under the accusation of a sinner with other sinners. The glorious One is covered with shame. The One who lives for ever has fallen a prey to death.[6]

Jesus' life in human flesh was an integral part of his atoning work, culminating in his sacrificial death. "Since therefore the children share *in flesh and blood*, he himself likewise *partook of the same things*, that through death he might destroy the one who has the power of death, that is, the devil, and deliver all those who through fear of death were subject to lifelong slavery" (Heb 2:14-15, emphasis added). In this way the Son became like us "in every respect, so that he might become a merciful and faithful high priest" who could uniquely offer himself in our stead (Heb 2:17).

In and through the incarnate Christ, God experiences human suffering, undergoing everything from misunderstandings to outright betrayal. In Christ, God knew temptation—not by way of distant, divine omniscience but by experience *as a man*, as a particular human being facing genuine temptation and struggle. Our challenges are not hypothetical to him. The first epistle of John observes three ways the "world" tries to draw us away from communion with God: "[1] the desires of the flesh and [2] the desires of the eyes and [3] pride of possessions" (1 Jn 2:16). Jesus, as the new and final Adam (1 Cor 15:45), confronts these temptations successfully and does not succumb to the evil one who attempted to seduce him in these three ways (Mt 4:1-11). Adam failed; Jesus did not.

Consistently the first three Gospels show the movement from Jesus' baptism to his wilderness temptation and then on to the beginning of his ministry (Mt 3:13–4:17; Mk 1:9-15; Lk 3:21–4:14). Accordingly, his time in the wilderness is our first indicator that Jesus' temptations represent all he will endure for us. Let us not think this episode was the only time Jesus was tempted. This initial event represents a larger, even cosmic fight going on throughout his ministry: the wilderness, Gethsemane, and ultimately Golgotha represent the whole. Golgotha serves as the climax of the struggle, not the start of it.

Jesus constantly dealt with human agony, sin, and misery in his own life, and therefore with judgment and death for all the years leading to his own death. This is why the Christian tradition so often speaks of Christ's *vicarious* life and death—he lived and died for us, in our place. The closer he gets to the cross, the more intense the challenges and pain become. At Gethsemane we read of Jesus in "earnest prayer": so heavy a weight were these trials that "his sweat became like great drops of blood falling down to the ground" (Lk 22:44). No one put it as powerfully as the author of Hebrews: "In the days of his flesh, Jesus offered up prayers and supplications, with loud cries and tears, to him who was able to save him from death, and he was heard because of his reverence" (Heb 5:7; cf. Mt 26:36-46). Jesus prayed not because he was fulfilling some bit part in a play for the local theater but out of his real suffering and in full dependence on his Father (Mk 14:36, 39). In his loneliness and physical weakness, as the storms were crashing all around him, Jesus rested on the promises and love of his Father.

Even as our hearts can be prone to question, filled with dread and doubt, let us take confidence that our God personally understands us, not hypothetically but concretely in Christ. Jesus wept tears, for in and through his incarnate life he had fully entered into the drama of fallen human experience. His ache and struggle give new meaning to our tears and suffering: God cares about our sin and distress so much that he enters into it himself.

Jesus identifies with us, not only in our beauty, not only in our grandeur, but especially in our vulnerability and temptation. At our worst, he knows us best. He knows what it is like to face questions, doubt, and loneliness when he was physically weak, exhausted, and exposed. So often when we find ourselves in vulnerable situations we easily give ourselves over to sinful desires, whether in the form of cultivating bitterness and envy or through fits of harmful self-indulgence. Jesus was tempted as we are—fully, consistently, truly—and those temptations took place in the flesh, in real time, under real pressures. Jesus, however, remained faithful during these temptations even amid his physical weakness and the jeers meant to cause him to doubt the Father's goodness and love (e.g., Mt 27:40-44; Lk 23:35-39).

Amid the pain of our own lives we commonly have to deal with powerful temptations and unnerving questions. Is God ignorant of or unconcerned with my pain? Are the circumstances of my life out of control and irrelevant to God? Does God care when I am mistreated and misunderstood by others amid my suffering? According to the gospel, Jesus—and thus God—knows and understands. "Because he himself suffered when tempted, he is able to help those who are being tempted" (Heb 2:18). This is no hollow gesture or empty promise. The temptations recorded for us in the Gospels normally arise when Jesus was not physically rested and strong but profoundly compromised. He understands those who struggle in weakness.

He prayed, he wept, he struggled, he was tempted, yet he remained always faithful. As we read in Hebrews, "Although he was a son, he *learned* obedience through what he suffered" (Heb 5:8). Here, the eternal Son of God did not presume upon his divine knowledge. From all eternity God knows everything, but he knows everything as eternal God. In sending the Son to become incarnate, something stunning happens: *God is able to know what it means to be tempted as a human, as a man, as a particular person.* Jesus does not know temptation by means of divine omniscience but from our side, the side of humanity. Bertrand Russell, in a very different context, once wrote an essay in which he made a distinction between what he called "knowledge by acquaintance" versus "knowledge by description."[7] We know things descriptively as we have no firsthand experience of the matter but learn of it indirectly, through some form of mediation. On the other hand, knowledge of acquaintance describes what we personally know directly, without an intermediary describing the reality. Put in these terms, God always descriptively understood the reality of human temptation, sin, and judgment. God knows everything. But only through the incarnate Son does God gain knowledge of the human experience by means of acquaintance—Jesus is tempted and experiences agony. He knows through personal experience what it is to laugh, experience sickness, miss loved ones who have died, feel let down by friends, and even suffer unjust harm. This is partly what is behind that statement that "he learned obedience through what he suffered."

Hebrews provides an unanticipated conclusion: "And being made perfect [through his sufferings], he became the source of eternal salvation" (Heb 5:9). Salvation is here linked to Jesus' whole life: his movement of solidarity *with* us concludes with his sacrificial death *for* us. Many stumble over the words *made perfect*, wondering how it is that Jesus the Son of God was not already perfect. *Perfect* here does not mean sinless, as if he were previously sinful, but refers rather to *fullness* or *completeness*. He lives a full or complete life, one filled with joy and delight, but also one plagued by pain and struggle.

His entire life anticipates Golgotha, where his suffering—physical, mental, emotional, and spiritual—reaches exhaustion. Eventually it causes his death. Jesus does not die spiritually in some abstract way. The Gospels clearly affirm that after horrible punishments and cruelty Jesus dies physically. He ceases to breathe. Blood and water pour from his side. He enters into the hole of death itself, the abyss to which all physical suffering points. In this way he is made complete in his sufferings, but as "complete" he is also uniquely able to offer himself for others.

BY HIS WOUNDS WE ARE HEALED

The Gospel writers present Jesus' ministry as holistic, bringing spiritual cleansing and physical healing as he embodies the Father's tender care in the power of the Spirit. Through him the Spirit of creation was moving about and starting the work of making all things new.

For example, Peter's mother-in-law was healed by Jesus' touch; her fever left, and she rose to serve him (Mt 8:15). After this healing occurred, people began to be brought to him, not only those with physical sickness but also those who suffered because they were "oppressed by demons." Through his actions and pronouncements we see into the heart of God's purposes: "He cast out the spirits with a word and healed all who were sick" (Mt 8:16). What we sometimes miss, however, is how the gospel connects this with Jesus' atoning work, as hinted at in Isaiah 53.[8] Matthew explains, "This was to fulfill what was spoken by the prophet Isaiah: 'He took our illnesses and bore our diseases'" (Mt 8:17). Isaiah had spoken on this coming "man of sorrows" who was "acquainted with grief"; *grief* here can just as easily be translated as "sickness" (Is 53:3).[9] In the context, *acquainted* doesn't just mean cognitive acknowledgement but experiential immersion: "he has borne our griefs [sickness] and carried our sorrows" (Is 53:4). The hurt of his people has became his own, so much so that it now belongs more to him than to them.

Our physical pain genuinely matters to Jesus—it matters to God! We are far too prone to spiritualize what Jesus makes physical, even theologizing his physical suffering into a response to a spiritual problem (sin), as if our true being were only spiritual and not physical. For Jesus, the physical and spiritual are indissolubly connected, and his life and death address them both. Notice that there seems to be something cumulative about his associations and suffering. He is absorbing the pain, the disease, the sickness, the death. He is absorbing it, experiencing it, embracing it. Basil the Great, speaking in fourth-century terms, argues that Christ was willing to go about "breathing [our sickness's] foul breath, that he may heal the sick."[10] And this he will carry all the way to the cross, ultimately being crushed by the sin and sickness of the world.

Christ's identification with us involves more than mere sympathy. In Isaiah's description of the suffering servant, his suffering is not merely like ours but has its cause, and its results, in us.[11]

> But he was wounded for *our* transgressions:
>> he was crushed for *our* iniquities;
> upon him was the chastisement that brought *us* peace,
>> and with his stripes *we* are healed. (Is 53:5, emphasis added)

He absorbs all of our brokenness and takes all our sin onto his own shoulders. Human sin brought with it a cosmic brokenness that fell under God's judgment (cf. Gen 3:14-19). God in Jesus takes upon himself the brokenness of fallen humanity (Gal 3:13; cf. Deut 21:23). To use Paul's words, "For our sake he made him to be sin who knew no sin, so that in him we might become the righteousness of God" (2 Cor 5:21).

In this passage Isaiah speaks of the servant as both an individual and a representative, both a singular person and a nation (Israel); that is, he could be both a man and Man.[12] The particular and the universal come together in Jesus, the new Adam. He will reverse the curse of the fall. In him alone is judgment carried out and death defeated; in him alone is healing and hope.

> All we like sheep have gone astray;
>> we have turned—every one—to his own way;
> and the LORD has laid on him
>> the iniquity of us all. (Is 53:6)

Isaiah shows that physical suffering and spiritual brokenness are entangled, and we need to appreciate that if we are to understand the significance of the Messiah's life and death.

This does not imply that your particular pain is related to some particular sin you have done. No. But the cosmic connection between human sin and a compromised creation—including our particular sufferings—is assumed throughout the story of Scripture. Only as this story is fully appreciated can we grasp the significance that the Son became one of us and on our behalf absorbed the full consequences of our sin.

The apostle Peter picked up this theme centuries after Isaiah lived, recognizing that Jesus fulfilled this Messianic role. Peter states that while Jesus himself "committed no sin" nor was deceitful in any way, he nevertheless was "reviled." Rather than respond to curses with curses, Jesus absorbed the suffering as he "continued entrusting himself to him who judges justly" (1 Pet 2:23). Jesus clearly understood these injustices against him within the larger context of a cosmic problem. The purpose of his incarnation and death was a cosmic redemption. He, in and through his body, becomes our hope and the hope of the whole world. "He himself bore our sins in his body on the tree, that we might die to sin and live to righteousness"; in this way he fulfilled the prophetic promise that "by his wounds you have been healed" (1 Pet 2:24; Is 53:4, 11). Like a literal shepherd seeking his lost sheep, the "Shepherd and Overseer of your souls" has come to rescue us.

He was oppressed, and he was afflicted,
> yet he opened not his mouth;
like a lamb that is led to the slaughter . . .
he was cut off out of the land of the living,
> stricken for the transgression of my people. (Is 53:7-8)

Isaiah and the Gospel writers say that Christ underwent his passion on behalf of others. The high priest became the sacrificial offering. He himself becomes the one mediator between God and "man." He did this by connecting himself intimately with us, so much so that his grave was associated with the wicked even though he himself was free from violence and deceit (Is 53:9).

Jesus carried our sin and sickness so that "his soul makes an offering for sin," with the result that his "offspring" shall live (Is 53:10). Only by his death could we know life and freedom. We needed to be unmade for the destruction of our sin and remade that we might live in him, and this is what he accomplished by bearing "our sins in his body on the tree" (1 Pet 2:24). As a result, we died in him and now live in him (2 Cor 5:14, 14; Gal 2:19-20). It was to achieve this that our representative willingly suffered on our behalf. "Out of the anguish of his soul he shall see and be satisfied," for this "servant" shall "make many to be accounted righteous," as "he shall bear their iniquities" (Is 53:11). This unique suffering servant who acts in solidarity and on behalf of others "poured out his soul to death and was numbered with the transgressors," with the result that "he bore the sin of many, and makes intercession" for them (Is 53:12). This one becomes not only one with us but one for us; one who embraces our sin and pain, absorbs the judgment associated with human rebellion, and brings hope.

Isaiah portrays all of this spiritual work in terms of physical embodiment. The spiritual and the physical are one. Our sin and death could not be overcome apart from concerns of the body precisely because we are not merely spiritual beings. In and through a real body, the body of the holy one, new life began where previously only death had had dominion. Theologian Paul L. Gavrilyuk writes that the ancient Christian perspective held that "God was not conquered by suffering" because "God's participation in suffering transformed the experience of suffering. In the incarnation God made human suffering his own . . . in order to transform suffering and redeem human nature."[13]

God is not interested in being eternally miserable: he enters suffering for the purpose of overcoming it, for the purpose of freeing us from the plague of our own sin and the cosmic consequences of human sin.[14] Jesus' story ends not with him as an eternal victim but as the eternal Lord who conquers sin and suffering in order to promise hope and renewal.

When we face our own aches, it is easy to lose confidence. Knowing this, the author of Hebrews points us to Jesus, the great revelation of God's holy and redeeming love. "We have confidence to enter the holy places by the blood of Jesus, by the new and living way that he opened for us through the curtain, that is through his flesh" (Heb 10:19-20). We marvel at God's astonishing condescension and life-giving action that takes place *through his flesh*. The author of Hebrews contends that if God in Christ was willing to take on our identity and act to rescue us, then we who are united to Christ by faith should come to him with confidence rather than dread.

> Let us draw near with a true heart in full assurance of faith, with our hearts sprinkled clean from an evil conscience and our bodies washed with pure water. Let us hold fast the confession of our hope without wavering, for he who promised is faithful. (Heb 10:22-23)

CONCLUSION

God can't taste dust, get sick, or become hungry. Nor can God die. Such events apply only to creatures that have bodies. Out of his love the Father sent his Son in the Spirit to take on genuine flesh, to become fully human. Only in this way can the eternal Lord—the God who cannot die—enter the reality of suffering and death. Only in this way can the God of light face the darkness of the devil. Only as incarnate can God enter the pit of the grave in order to fill it with life. His death encompasses both the physical and the spiritual aspects of his humanity in their unity. Jesus physically suffered, and Jesus actually died.

Jesus' substitutionary life and death change everything for us, for he is the great revelation of the eternal God's love and commitment to us. "All the promises of God find their Yes in him" (2 Cor 1:20). When the pain of our suffering overwhelms us, when the confusion of broken relationships warps our vision and threatens to crush us in despair, when unrealized hopes now seem only to taunt us, we look to the suffering servant who became one with us and offered himself in our place. And in so doing, he changed the narrative and the reality of the world. He brought light to the darkness, life to death, hope to despair. In him everything does look different, even our sickness and grief.

We began this chapter by wondering if God cares about our physical suffering. Is it just when we face persecution that our sufferings matter? We wondered if there is any real connection between our suffering and that of Christ. The connection underlies the entire gospel story of Jesus' life. His was a life filled with trials and temptations and concluded with his physical death. In his incarnation Jesus became one of us so that his life, death, and resurrection would apply to us, destroying our sin and death and replacing it with new life. Thus we live by faith in union with our risen King.

The church, which serves as the body of Christ on earth, now expresses God's transformative presence and love in a cross-centered way. As the body of Christ we now understand suffering corporately: when one hurts, we all hurt; when one struggles, we all struggle; when one falls short, we all fall. This is *our* pain, *our* challenge, and *our* ache because all of this is included in why the Son became incarnate and was willing to face even death on our behalf.

As the body of Christ we "complete the sufferings of Christ" by living from *his* life in his confrontation with our world. Our present sin and sufferings are part of what he died for. Jesus continues to touch the wounded and bring healing through us. These episodes in his ministry, and ultimately what was accomplished by the cross, provide us with a true taste of shalom.

As the body of Christ we participate by the Spirit in God's present work: through our entering into one another's sufferings he rekindles our longing for a time when shalom will be unhindered, when sin and suffering will be no more. Empowered by the Spirit we bear one another's offenses and sorrows, bringing words of encouragement and grace because we are secure in the shadow of the cross (1 Thess 5:9-11).

The apostle Paul connects our sufferings with the sufferings of Christ, and this provides a basis for us to encourage one another amid our pain:

> Blessed be the God and Father of our Lord Jesus Christ, the Father of mercies and God of all comfort, who comforts us in all our affliction, so that we may be able to comfort those who are in any affliction, with the comfort with which

we ourselves are comforted by God. For as we share abundantly in Christ's sufferings, so through Christ we share abundantly in comfort too. (2 Cor 1:3-5)

Because God comforts us in our suffering we are able to extend his comfort to others. As the "love of Christ controls us" (2 Cor 5:13-15), we point the wounded to the incarnate and risen Son and to our unity with him. So now we experience our physical suffering as linked to the sufferings of Jesus—his life and death mean that these painful afflictions will not be the final word.

Our sufferings must always be understood through his. Thus our anguish can return us to grace and healing; by faith we see that these pains point not merely to brokenness but to a good creation that has been compromised, and to an even better Creator who has come to renew creation and set it free.

8

RISEN AND REMAINING

*For as by a man came death, by a man has come
also the resurrection of the dead.*

1 CORINTHIANS 15:21

*Beggars, receive your food; you who are palsied and maimed in the body,
received the medicine for your ills. For through the hope of the resurrection,
virtue is sought out and vice is hated, whereas if the resurrection is taken
away, one saying will be found to prevail in all: Let us eat and drink, for
tomorrow we die.*

GREGORY OF NYSSA, *PASCHAL SERMON*

*Christians are Easter people living from and toward
that Easter experience of a new creation.*

HANS SCHWARZ, *THE HUMAN BEING*

What do you really believe about God, about purpose, and about
hope, and what do you believe about how our bodies fit into your perspective
on these things? We begin here with two stories that ask the same questions.

WHAT IF GOD IS DEAD?

Lighting a lantern as the morning sun rose, a "madman" made his way to the marketplace where others were beginning their day.[1] His voice rose, shrieking, "I seek God! I seek God!" Those who heard the man didn't believe in God; they had moved beyond such childish fairy tales. They smiled as they watched the madman, finding him not simply crazy but hilarious. Blissfully they taunted the seeker:

> Has [God] got lost? asked one. Did he lose his way like a child? asked another. Or is he hiding? Is he afraid of us? Has he gone on a voyage? Emigrated? Thus they yelled and laughed.

Rather than be intimidated, the madman "jumped into their midst and pierced them with his eyes." He had questions for the crowd, just as they did for him.

> "Whither is God?" he cried; "I will tell you. We have killed him—you and I. All of us are his murderers. But how did we do this? How could we drink up the sea?"

His questions continued as he spun out the logic implied by the crowd's assumption that it is folly to believe God exists. To them, God was nothing more than the figment of primitive man's imagination: there is no deity; no One ruled the world.

Like a magician pulling a rabbit out of a hat, to the surprise of all, the madman then demonstrates who is actually mad! It is not he but the crowd who is living in an illusion. They laugh at the idea that God can be found, that God is alive. And yet they assume that their lives have meaning, purpose, and logic. He taunts the *un*believers: "Are we not straying as through an infinite nothing? Do we not feel the breath of empty space? Has it not become colder? Is not night continually closing in on us?"

God is dead, and "we have killed him." Shocking to many, what we discover is that a genuinely "godless" world has no grasp on liberty and joy but is necessarily subject to meaninglessness and fear. The awful realization takes shape slowly, but unless our understanding of the difference between *good* and *evil* has some transcendent anchor, that understanding becomes a blur, then darkness.[2] If there is no God, then no One is listening. No One cares. Love, beauty, honor, and reality have lost their moorings. Now these once-assumed virtues threaten to fly off like balloons slipping from the hands of a naive child who thought it would be fun to let them go, believing they could easily be caught again. Instead, of course, they float away into the sky and are gone.

Having more wisdom than the rest, the madman concluded that if there were no deity, then meaning, forgiveness, and hope are mere vapors. He does not relent but continues to press his listeners until they understand him. "How shall we comfort ourselves, the murderers of all murderers? . . . who will wipe this blood off us?"

If humanity killed God—if the Holy One *never* was—then redemption is not possible. Pain has no meaning. Betrayal, lies, selfishness, greed, and lust—there can be no criticism of these, even if we hurt others in the process. Everything is reduced to strength and power.[3] So what do we do with guilt? "What water is there for us to clean ourselves? What festivals of atonement, what sacred games shall we invent?" In fact, by killing God, humanity has itself become god, or gods.

Before the coming of the madman, the people had failed to be honest about the implications of their unbelief. They had failed to live out their unfaith, their uncreed, their disbelief in God. The madman demanded honesty—unflinching honesty.

"Here the madman fell silent and looked again at his listeners; and they, too, were silent and stared at him in astonishment." After a time of silence, he threw down his lantern to its destruction and declared, "I have come too early." It was clear to him that while they claimed there was no God, they were still living on the borrowed capital of Christianity. They had clung to a desire for cosmic purpose despite having dethroned cosmic order. If indeed God is dead, then putting off worries about a distant heaven and hell are not the only consequences.

The madman understood what all the others had not: the absence of God has everything to do with *this* life, with the present, with our struggle to find meaning *now*. And for our purposes, this has everything to do with our pain, our hurts, our fears, and our hopes.

This story, told by the nineteenth-century philosopher Friedrich Nietzsche, is sobering indeed. Although we reject Nietzsche's atheism, we can at least applaud his honesty about the consequences of such a God-denying conclusion.

Let us now consider another story, an older one.

AN EMPTY TOMB?

On the cross we see vulnerability and weakness. The crowd flings taunts at Jesus like rocks: "He saved others, he cannot save himself" (Mk 15:31). Not simply those authorities who hanged him on the cross but even his fellow cross bearers "reviled him" (Mk 15:32).

Even many that had earlier followed Jesus and his message thought his death was the end. Despair and disillusionment replaced courage and purpose. The Nazarene's own last words raise concern about being forsaken by God (Mk 15:34).

Jesus is dead. God's silence terrifies. Like a dense fog, the dominance of the mundane begins to roll back in—the need for shelter, food, tears, and labor.

Some still believed, still hoped, even if it was unclear how well they understood what had happened or might happen. Joseph of Arimathea was such a figure.[4] Joseph, who had begun to seek the "the kingdom of God, *took courage* and went to Pilate" (Mk 15:43, emphasis added). But what did Joseph want? The "*body* of Jesus" (Mk 15:43, emphasis added). Convinced that the body of Christ should be treated with dignity, Joseph took a risk. He asked Pilate, and because he was respected, Pilate entertained his request. But it appears Pilate was "surprised to hear that [Jesus] should have already died" (Mk 15:44). How easy it was to only imagine Jesus as strong, even threatening. Jesus once had multitudes of followers, and it looked like they were growing in numbers. Pilate had heard reports of miracles, healings, and signs. Jesus seemed unafraid, unwilling to play political games, whether civil or religious. He seemed so strong. But *now*, where was his strength? He was but another dead body; a body in need of a burial. Once Pilate confirmed his death—it was still hard to believe—he gave him to Joseph, who would give him to the grave. A heavy stone was rolled over the tomb's entrance.

The stone signaled a kind of finality. The King of the Jews was no more. No King. No kingdom. Just fanciful dreams.

Some of his followers gave thought to Jesus' body in that grave. The dead deserved a certain kind of care: a washing, application of spices, wrapping in grave cloths. But when the women arrived two days after the burial, the stone had been rolled away—sunlight was breaking into the once dark tomb.

What did they see? Not the body of their Master. Jesus was gone. But one "dressed in a white robe" was sitting nearby. Witnessing their dismay, he declares, "Do not be alarmed. You seek Jesus of Nazareth, who was crucified. *He has risen;* he is not here" (Mk 16:6, emphasis added). The man then tells them to go, to let Peter and others know. Jesus will meet them in Galilee: "There you will see him" (Mk 16:7).

Then, in the final words of the Gospel of Mark, we read a stunning end to the story: "And they went out and fled from the tomb, for trembling and astonishment had seized them, and they said nothing to anyone, for they were afraid" (Mk 16:8).[5]

Remarkably, Mark's Gospel ends not by explaining everything, not by answering all of the questions, but instead by presenting the reader with a clear yet unspoken question: *If Jesus has risen, what does that mean?* Why might it be that they responded with "trembling and astonishment"? Why would it be appropriate for the last word of the Gospel—the *good news*—to be the word *afraid*? "They were *afraid*." What is so frightening, even worthy of astonishment?

Mark provokes in his readers unsettling questions: if the crucified and buried Jesus is alive, what does that mean about Jesus? About God? About humanity? About our bodies? About me?

CONSEQUENCES OF BELIEF

The philosopher Friedrich Nietzsche and the writer of Mark's Gospel have much in common here. Both authors tell powerful stories. Both call their listeners to some form of faith, or, more precisely, they both reveal that their readers are already living in a state of conflicted faith, and both writers call for their readers to choose. One demands that his readers affirm the cold emptiness that must accompany the freedom from divine presence and concern that they have already embraced; the other encourages his readers to embrace the God who has come near to us as one of us. This Jesus, God's Son, is not merely compassionate but powerful—even more authoritative than death itself. He rose from the grave. Which story do you believe?

Many in Nietzsche's day naively imagined that denying or ignoring God leads to human liberty. But his madman reveals the inevitable to his listeners: denying divine personal presence, governance, and power leads not to human peace and harmony but to anarchy. By killing one *Almighty*, countless small *mighties* seek to declare themselves: in the end it is not goodness or beauty or truth, but simply raw human power that rules, or, as becomes clear, fails to rule. The madman reveals a frightening world in which not simply death but life itself is to be feared.

Nietzsche's narrative of the madman surprises many readers, for many assume that the message is directed *against* Christians. The real target of this particular diatribe, however, is not the saint—who he still believes is living in an illusion—but the naive *non*believers who think they can deny divine presence and yet retain transcendent meaning. Unlike contemporary trends such as the "new atheism," which eerily sounds like the villagers mocking the madman, Nietzsche faced the implications of godlessness: without God we are alone, left to create meaning for ourselves. To Nietzsche's credit, he is willing to be an honest broker—if there is no God, then we should stop pretending and acknowledge the dark abyss. Such a conclusion has profound implications for how we view our bodies, deal with pain, and understand death itself.

For the Christian the great testimony of divine presence and power is the incarnation and resurrection of Jesus the Messiah. We have already considered how the life and death of Christ should inform our view of faith and suffering, but now we turn to the significance of the empty tomb. Without this resurrection, the injustices, cruelty, disparity, pain, suffering, and heartache of this world would undo us. But in light of the life, death, and resurrection of Christ we are able to confront the pain of this world and defiantly proclaim, "This is not how it is supposed to be" and "This is not how it will be." Thus we now turn to the all-important resurrection.

DO NOT BE AFRAID . . . BUT WORSHIP

Mark's Gospel ends with the word *afraid*; as they leave the empty tomb, the women are "afraid." If Jesus has risen, what are the implications? Matthew, however, takes his readers further. We open the last chapter of Matthew's Gospel also with an empty tomb, again with "an angel of the Lord" who was "like lightning" with clothing "white as snow" (Mt 28:2-3). But what does the angel say to them? "Do *not* be afraid." Why? "For I know that you seek Jesus who was crucified. He is not here, for he has risen, as he said" (Mt 28:5-6).

Matthew's account agrees with Mark's—they leave the empty tomb now "with fear." But this Gospel takes the story further. Matthew observes that those present experienced not just one feeling but a swirl of emotions: "They departed quickly from the tomb with fear *and great joy.*" Why pick between fear and joy? The Gospels don't ask us to; in fact, they recognize that if we understand and believe their narrative, we also will feel some combination of fear and joy.

What do they do next? They run.

As they ran to tell the disciples they actually end up running into Jesus. Part of what then appears to unnerve them is how ordinary, how everyday it was: "Jesus met them." Offering a familiar and warm salute, Jesus simply says, "Greetings!" (Mt 28:8-9). The last time they had seen their Master, he was bloody and badly beaten; now he is standing before them, alive, well, and whole. His welcome seems modest given the stark reversal of this encounter.

Seeing the risen Jesus, what do the disciples do? They want to touch his body! "They came up and *took hold of his feet* and *worshiped him*" (v. 9, emphasis added). As good and faithful Jews, they know you only worship the One living God, Yahweh. Yet now, this man, this particular human creature, is discovered to be somehow, none other than the "Author of life"—the Creator (Acts 3:15). Jesus is recognized as the Word of God, from whom, through whom, and for whom all things are made (cf. Jn 1:1; 1 Cor 8:6; Col 1:16). Thus, the disciples can't help themselves: they necessarily worship. They are on holy ground before the Holy One. They identify Jesus as somehow within the one divine identity.[6] They may not fully understand, but they understand enough to worship. Touch. Bow. Identify. And *worship*.

Jesus responds: "Do not be afraid" (Mt 28:10). He then reestablishes his connection by identifying with them: "Tell my brothers . . . they will see me" (v. 10).[7] Seeing Jesus—his *physical* appearance—drew them to worship. Not abstractions, not empty ideas, but the real physical presence of this particular One provokes them to worship. Others had been healed, and Jesus had even resuscitated some people from the dead (Mt 9:25; Lk 7:13-15; Jn 11:43-44).[8] Yet no one *worshiped* those other people. Something was different with this empty tomb.

Jesus was raised by the Father's love in the power of the Spirit; this Jesus was not just a raised creature but the risen Lord (cf. Jn 2:21; Rom 4:24; 10:9; 1 Pet 1:21). Raised and freed from corruption, this Jesus becomes the anchor of our forgiveness of sins and promised renewed communion with God (Acts 13:30-39; Rom 6:3-5). By his resurrection Jesus was uniquely recognized as being within the one divine identity. Jesus was none other than the

Son of Man, the one given "dominion and glory and a kingdom" that will be everlasting and never destroyed (Dan 7:14; Mt 17:9; Lk 9:22). This exalted heavenly figure Daniel spoke of was now identified as the risen Jesus who had come to renew his creation and rescue his people.[9]

OUR HESITATION

"But some doubted" (Mt 28:17). This detail demonstrates the author's deep realism (resurrection confuses people) and confidence (such a Lord as this resolves such doubts). Two competing responses seem to be put together: "They worshiped him, *but some doubted*," or it could be translated "some hesitated." Why or what is it they doubt? They "see" Jesus, so their hesitation is not about his physical presence. No, the doubt or hesitation is about the worship. Some begin to worship, and they are worshiping one who is staring right back at them through human eyes. What does this say about God's identity, about his commitment to his creation in general and humanity in particular?

To glorify and worship any other than the true God would have been considered blasphemous and punishable by stoning. But now the disciples were looking at Jesus, their former rabbi, their teacher and friend; only this Jesus did not appear to be merely their earthly master but, to echo Thomas's stunning confession, Jesus is recognized as "My Lord and my God" (Jn 20:28; cf. Rom 1:4). Any person encountering God should respond with worship. Thus the apparent dilemma: worship the risen Jesus or not? There is no neutrality. But those who worship a risen Savior discover God's intention for their bodies and what the gospel means for their present suffering.

Only as we look at the resurrected Jesus can we find courage to live through our pain, questions, and struggles. Looking at the risen Messiah we are brought to worship the one God who so loved his people that he became one of his people, took on true flesh and blood, including our pains, hunger, and weakness. He took it all the way to the grave. And then in the power of the Spirit of God he rose from the dead to declare God's great victory over sin, death, and the devil. This same Spirit of God is then poured out on us, securing our eventual bodily resurrection (Rom 8:11). Looking at the risen Christ we discover the depth of God's love, his solidarity with us, and his compassionate power, which will make all things new through Jesus, the firstborn from the dead. Hesitations should cease, and worship should begin.

JESUS' RESURRECTION IS A BODILY RESURRECTION

Over the past century it has become fairly common for some modern biblical scholars to assert that Jesus did not physically rise from the grave.[10] These resurrection stories, some believe, were mere myths meant to point to an existential truth about humanity, not to tell you about a historical event. Instead, the "resurrection" mentioned in the Scriptures simply points to new hopes and new possibilities that arise in our hearts as inspired by stories about Jesus; they tell us we do not need to believe a man literally rose from the dead.[11]

The apostles themselves display a very different view. As the apostle Paul proclaims, "If Christ has not been raised, then our preaching is in vain and your faith is in vain" (1 Cor 15:14). The apostolic proclamation about Jesus' lordship and his abiding significance clearly requires an affirmation of a bodily resurrection of Jesus.[12] If there is no physical resurrection, then by all means, let us eat, drink, and distract ourselves from the meaningless pain and struggle (1 Cor 15:32). Jesus himself displays his purpose, connecting his death and resurrection: "I lay down my life that I may take it up again" (Jn 10:17). In other words, his rising from the grave is not meant as an interesting but disconnected event. As George Eldon Ladd concludes, Jesus' resurrection is "the essential completion of his death. Resurrection is the purpose of his death."[13]

Bodily resurrection (Jesus' and ours!) is an essential assertion for catholic orthodoxy.[14] This book shows that Jesus' bodily resurrection is indispensable for providing genuine comfort and hope to those who face chronic pain and various disorders, and who ultimately endure all the marks of death's taunting presence. If Jesus never rose from the tomb, then only the voice of decay speaks truth. But if Jesus did indeed rise, then his voice speaks through and over our pain and struggle.

SEE AND TOUCH

Luke's Gospel also clearly asserts Jesus' physical resurrection. On the first day of the week, Jesus' followers find his tomb empty and proclaim that he has "risen" (Lk 24:1-12; esp. v. 6). After a mysterious and fascinating conversation with a few people on the road to Emmaus (Lk 24:13-35, esp. v. 27; cf. v. 45),[15] Jesus later comes to his disciples who had gathered together to talk about recent events. He startles them with his declaration "Peace to you!" (Lk 24:36). Luke explains that some there were "startled" because they "thought they saw a spirit" (v. 37). How tempting and convenient that option would be for Luke, to explain Jesus' "appearing" as nothing more than a phantasm, a hovering disembodied spirit. But that is not what Luke reports.

Jesus asks them, "Why are you troubled, and why do doubts arise in your hearts?" Then, rather than offering a philosophical explanation, Jesus offers his body. "See my hands and my feet, that it is I myself. Touch me, and see. For a spirit does not have flesh and bones as you see that I have" (Lk 24:38-39). Flesh and bones! Similarly, in his postresurrection encounter with Thomas, he offers him physical confirmation: "Put your finger here, and see my hands; and put out your hand, and place it in my side. Do not disbelieve, but believe" (Jn 20:27).

The risen Messiah does not shed his flesh but shows God's affirmation of his creation by continuing to live in the flesh. The Messiah is physically raised from the dead. Jesus is still Jesus! In fact, after showing them his hands and feet, he asked them for food; a ghost does not eat broiled fish, but Jesus "took it and ate before them" (Lk 24:43). What is so remarkable is that these actions are so ordinary, so earthy.

SIMILAR, AND YET . . .

Jesus is the same, yet something is different. As N. T. Wright observes, the Gospels present the risen Jesus as "a firmly embodied human being whose body possesses new, unexpected and unexplained characteristics."[16] Struggling to find adequate language, Wright speaks of Jesus' "trans-physicality" or "transformed physicality." Jesus' risen body is clearly the same body—with the marks of the wounds in his side, his hands, his body. He eats, speaks, touches. But he is free of pain, having overcome death itself. This matters not merely for our understanding of the risen Messiah but for appreciating the Christian hope of resurrection. Jesus is the same, yet different.[17] So it will be for us.

An early church father, Didymus of Alexandria (313–398)—sometimes known as Didymus the Blind in the ancient world—reflected carefully on Paul's promises in 1 Corinthians 15. Didymus appreciated that this "new creation" of resurrection was not meant to obliterate us but to *renew* us in Christ. The point is that this is the same person, with the same body: "Somehow, then, what is raised is both other than and the same as the body that perishes."[18] The analogy Didymus uses here is of an infant who grows into a child or even an adult. These are not two different people but one and the same, not "two subjects or two persons, but only one, in two different stages." The Jesus who rose is the same as the Jesus who died, only now he is glorified. So it will be with us. We rise, but then we will be free from sin and suffering, including physical pain. The same, yet different.

This makes me think a friend, who, as we talked about the resurrection, could not keep a smile from his face. After we reflected together, I ended up asking him to write a brief letter explaining what he told me. I prefer that you hear this in his words, rather than mine. Here is what he sent me:

> I am a congenital heart patient with several skeletal issues that necessitate that I ambulate on crutches every day of my life. From birth, my life has been significantly impacted by physical disability, and I have undergone a number of surgical operations to improve the use of my heart and legs; nevertheless, nothing in this world of modern medicine has been able to or will be able to fully heal my body and make it whole. I have never known a day that I did not bear a 6" scar on my chest that reminds me that I should not be alive, nor have I ever walked the length of a table without crutches or knelt on bended knee (something that my fused knees cannot do). I have never knelt in prayer, and if the Lord should one day bring a woman into my life, I would have to sit down in order to ask her to be my bride.
>
> Yet, these realities point to my greater need of being restored spiritually to fellowship with my heavenly Father, before whom I am hopelessly disabled by my sin apart from His work to redeem me through Christ. I view my disabilities as reminders of my utter dependence upon Christ for salvation and life, and am sure that in eternity He will restore me to wholeness. By carrying me through the trials in my life, He has given me a longing for the coming new creation, when He will restore me physically as I behold Him in restored communion unhindered by my sin (which He will have eradicated forever).
>
> The coming resurrection gives me hope that a day is coming when I will be made like Christ, and freed from the curse of sin. Secondarily, I rejoice in the hope that He will give me the gift of a resurrected body free from the physical infirmities I have wrestled with my whole life. There will be a day when I will be able to bend my knee, and the first time that I do so will be at the feet of Jesus when I see Him face to face and bow before Him as His redeemed child. On that day I will love and embrace Him with a resurrected heart made whole by His touch, and freed from the power of death forever. Oh, for that day to come!

My friend will be the same person he is now, only he will be free not simply from the grief of sin and sorrow but from physical aches and pain. Here is one who instinctually connects body and soul, pain and praise, lament and longing. His physical freedom is coming, but that day is not yet.

SAVED FROM WHAT?

As Christians we often talk about being saved. Salvation is found frequently and powerfully in biblical language and imagery. But once in a while we should slow down and ask, What are we saved *from*? Throughout the Scriptures this imagery of salvation conveys many things. God's people are saved from their oppressors (e.g., Ex 14:30; Deut 33:29; Ps 18:3), from the tyranny of poverty (e.g., Ps 34:6), from their ignorance (Is 45:14-25), and even from their own sin, which has compromised their experience of resting in God's kind countenance (e.g., Ps 80). The Son of God saves us from the great enemies of sin, death, and the devil. For our purposes I would like to highlight here the one that is easily forgotten during times of prosperity and peace but always returns at some point for God's people, corporately and individually.

We are saved *from the tyranny of death*. As Paul vividly puts it, "The last enemy to be destroyed is death" (1 Cor 15:26). Our aches and suffering reach a climax in our death—it is what all our pain points to: our strength will ultimately give out, our breath cease, and our body become lifeless. Yet to this apparent final word, the Word comes and breathes new life. This Word, which originally spoke the world into existence, now promises that he will raise us from death to life—not metaphorically but physically.

Jesus the risen Lord overcame death, and by his life-giving Spirit we now approach death as those who need not despair, for death no longer has the final word. That is why Christians are told not to grieve "as others do who have no hope" (1 Thess 4:13). Death does not define us, life does: *his* risen and remaining life. Fear of death does not crush us, for Jesus rose. This does not mean we ignore our current struggles and pain, nor does it imply that we shouldn't deeply feel the loss of loved ones when they die. But because of the resurrection, the darkness of death is not the final word—we have hope.

We are saved from the finality of death. We will rise. True Christian hope is not based on the immortality of the soul but on promised bodily resurrection. We are saved from the despondency that imagines our aches and pains, our labored breath, and our fading memories will be the end. We are saved from death; or maybe better, we are saved *through* death, by the death and resurrection of Christ, for though we die, yet we will live (Jn 11:25).

Here we are reminded of the sneers aimed at Jesus as he hung on the cross: "He saved others; he cannot save himself" (Mt 27:42; Mk 15:31; Lk 23:35). Ironically, the only way he could secure their salvation and eternal life was *not* by saving himself but instead by giving himself over unto death. Only by his death and resurrection could he secure the life of others (Rom 5:10). Offering great comfort to the believer, Paul concludes, "Thanks be to God, who gives us the victory [over death and sin] through our Lord Jesus Christ" (1 Cor 15:57). But this victory, secured by the death and resurrection of Jesus, will not be fully experienced until we are raised.

Jesus was interested in much more than providing temporary resuscitation—all whom he raised, including Lazarus, would die again. Nor was his pledge of "eternal life" meant to be an endless life of pain and suffering: that had never been God's promise. Such everlasting life would not be a gift but a curse. Rather, the Son of God promised a new life, eternal life, life ultimately liberated from sin and the corresponding curse (cf. Jn 5:26-29); a resurrection life free to worship the triune God and free from the consequences of sin and death.

JESUS, OUR ASCENDED HIGH PRIEST

We anticipate the eventual renewal of heaven on earth, including the resurrection of the dead. But for now, that new creation is not yet realized, and so we wait. In the midst of our present pain, however, we are mindful that we have a sympathetic high priest in the heavens who fully appreciates our humanity and weakness.

Hebrews 7 gives the promise that Jesus holds a permanent priesthood, because "he continues forever" (Heb 7:24). Jesus did not merely rise from the grave but ascended into the heavens and even now is at the right hand of God (Lk 22:69; Acts 2:33; 5:31; Heb 1:3). For the author of Hebrews this is a great comfort, because it means that Jesus is uniquely able to "save to the uttermost those who draw near to God" (Heb 7:25). Such promised salvation is whole or complete in Christ. He is not merely interested in saving some part of a person but saving the whole person, and saving them completely.

Further, the author says, "Since he always lives to make intercession for them" (Heb 7:25; cf. Rom 8:34). We often read this text and immediately paint a picture of Jesus in heaven constantly praying for us.

Unfortunately, that reading often ends up presenting a problematic picture, with the ascended Jesus pleading with his Father to love us, and the Father only reluctantly giving into those unceasing prayers. As if we should believe that if it were up to the Father, he would destroy us all. Well, if that is how we understand Jesus' heavenly intercession, then we have grave problems in our view of God. This scene pits the Father against the Son, viewing the Son as full of compassion and love, and the Father as consumed with wrath. It isn't difficult to show that this goes against what the Scriptures actually teach. The Father so loved the world that he sent his Son, in the power of the Spirit, so that salvation might be achieved (Jn 3:16). Salvation is an act of the triune God (cf. 1 Cor 12:4-6; 2 Cor 13:14; Gal 4:6; 1 Pet 1:1-2). Jesus' heavenly intercession is the fruit of God's love, not the reason for his love. We should never pit the persons of the Trinity against one another.

When we read that the ascended Jesus "always lives to make intercession" for God's people (Heb 7:25), I would encourage us to see that Jesus as mediator is our connection to God (1 Tim 2:5). In other words, Jesus embodies our need and dependence before God just as he embodies God's love for us. God's commitment to his people occurs in this body not simply when the Son assumes a human nature in the womb of Mary but also when, after his death and resurrection, he ascends in this body to the throne room of God. *The ongoing presence of the incarnate Christ is the intercession.* He is the mediator; he is the embodied prayer; he himself always lives to be the intercession.

John Owen, the seventeenth-century Puritan theologian, reminds us to keep the whole gospel story in mind, from incarnation to death, from resurrection to ascension. This is one story, one truth, and we should avoid separating these events.[19] In particular, we are prone to neglect the ascension, forgetting that the ascended Jesus *remains* our *incarnate* Lord.[20] "It is a fundamental article of faith," Owen argues, "that he is in the same body in heaven wherein he conversed here on earth; as well as the faculties of his rational soul are continued the same in him."[21] The divine and human natures are perfectly united in the one person of Jesus in an unbreakable union. As Hilary of Poitiers (310–367) concluded, "By assuming flesh . . . [the Son] acquired our nature in our totality, and became all that we are, but did not lose that which He was before."[22] The Son was and remains fully God, but with the incarnation, he is now and always fully human.

That Jesus *continues to be human* even now—at the right hand of God—is fundamental to his securing our salvation.'[23] Questions about how and where his body might be are for another discussion,[24] but our Lord's full humanity means that he has a physical body and is in that manner our eternal Mediator and Lord.[25] "The body which was pierced is that which all eyes shall see, and no other."[26]

In addition to passages that describe our heavenly King as seated at the right hand of God (e.g., Lk 22:69; Col 1:3; Heb 1:3; 1 Pet 3:22), there are a few passages that describe him as standing. His standing shows he is always alert, concerned, and ready to receive his own (Acts 7:55-56). And as the messianic Son of Man who has now been crucified, risen, and ascended into the heavens, he also serves as a judge and advocate, having the authority to forgive sins and offer final shalom (Dan 7:13-14; Ps 110:1; cf. Lk 5:24; 6:22). He stands for his people, representing his care and eternal provision; he is their King and Lord, the one who watches his servants and rises to show grace and true hospitality to his children who face the threat of death.

TAKE COURAGE AND LIVE

Christian affirmation of resurrection is not chiefly about escaping this world but righting it. Resurrection is not about denying this world but rather enabling believers to have an honest assessment of their experience and yet to have a real hope for restoration beyond it. Pain is real, but it is not the only reality.

Nietzsche is right: if God is really dead, if we really killed him, then the dynamics of the world can be explained in terms of power. But the resurrection changes our analysis: apparent weakness can be the face of true strength. You can even be willing to die, to lay down your life for others, because you—not just your ideas but *you*—shall rise.

The incarnation and cross were never meant merely to indicate divine empathy but also to be divine provision. Jesus lives with a purpose: as the firstborn from the dead, he renews creation and promises a future of shalom. None of this holds true, however, if the physical resurrection and ascension of Jesus the Messiah didn't happen. His bodily resurrection is key: the hope for humanity and for the world is a material hope for a re-created world.

We must never forget that God is not embarrassed by his creation, but he is renewing it from the inside out. Redemption does not merely right us psychologically, bringing some kind of emotional calm to our stormy dispositions. Some psychological models of Christian spirituality fall short when they focus all of their attention on a person's internal landscape, failing to fully appreciate that the Christian life is one of embodied relationships. What is happening and will happen with our bodies is crucial to who we are and what God is doing.

The crucified and risen Christ is our only avenue to renewed love for God and neighbor. His resurrection was not merely a blip on a historical time line but rather an in-breaking of the future, in which the infinite God took to himself the brokenness and sin of this world and then crushed it, demonstrating a promised future of shalom for those who are now connected to the risen Christ (Gal 2:20). Our current pain and anticipated death do not define us. Christ does.

CONCLUSION

Christ's resurrection establishes and foreshadows our own eventual bodily resurrection. Thus the substance and meaning of our lives are not confined to our present circumstances; we live in the now and not yet, between the coming of the kingdom and the full realization of that kingdom. United to Christ, Christians have not only died with him but have also risen with him in his resurrection (Rom 6:8; Col 2:12; 3:1-4) and will rise to him in our own resurrections. Because this risen Christ now lives in the heavens, and because he has united himself with us, he continues to break into our lives, assuring us that we will never be separated from him and shaping our vision for our lives (Col 3:1).

Why was a real bodily resurrection necessary? The Father sent the Son in the power of the Spirit not simply to visit the earth but to renew the earth and rescue his fallen people. Augustine said, "His resurrection from the dead . . . was a sufficient indication that no part of human nature is lost, since they are all safe in God's keeping."[27] This is a great comfort to us when we feel like our bodies betray us, when the aches never leave, and when mourning threatens to overwhelm our souls. During such times we need to echo those words confessed by the church through the ages: Christ has died. Christ has risen. Christ will come again.

PART III

LIFE TOGETHER

9

FAITH, HOPE, AND LOVE

I believe that I shall look upon the goodness of the L<small>ORD</small>
in the land of the living!
Wait for the L<small>ORD</small>*;*
be strong, let your heart take courage;
wait for the L<small>ORD</small>*!*

P<small>SALM</small> 27:13-14

I love the Lord, because he has heard
my voice and my pleas for mercy.
Because he inclined his ear to me,
therefore I will call on him as long as I live.

P<small>SALM</small> 116:1-2

The apostle Paul concludes his meditation on love with the words
"So now faith, hope, and love abide, these three; but the greatest of these is love"
(1 Cor 13:13).[1] This is a "still more excellent way" than the path of contention
and self-promotion that the Corinthian church was pursuing (1 Cor 12:31). We
are able to live as those who are strengthened in faith, encouraged by hope,

and governed by love. This triplet of theological virtues connects to key Christian images, most especially incarnation, cross, resurrection, and feast. We have already spent time on the first three as we considered how, in Christ, God is both with us (incarnation), for us (cross), and able to transform our suffering to bring new life (resurrection). We will later discuss our invitation to participate in the Lord's Supper (feast), which is a foretaste of our ultimate freedom and hope.

Together these words and images are vital for Christians, not only as we proclaim the story of the gospel but also as we live within that story. Living within this story means that we strengthen our weakened sisters and brothers by drawing them to and reminding them of the word, presence, and action of the triune God, becoming avenues of God's grace and mercy. Life as God's people thus becomes the environment that sustains and nourishes those who suffer. Consequently, our examination of suffering will be holistic, with concern for body and soul, mind and will, doubt and promise, frustration and love. Only such a holistic assessment will be faithful both to the cross and to the resurrection of our Lord; thus we maintain a realistic and honest assessment of the pain, and the radical and subversive hope that declares our present suffering is not all there is. The Christian life requires not an individual but a people—the people of God. Only together can we believe, hope, and love amid our struggles.

FAITH

> I believe; help my unbelief! (Mk 9:24)

Søren Kierkegaard, in his provocative work *Fear and Trembling*, retells the story of Abraham. In his epilogue to that story Kierkegaard repeatedly claims "faith is the highest passion in a person." "No generation," he observes, "begins at any other point than where the previous one did."[2] His observation is that while one can grow up in close proximity to the Christian religion, hearing its stories and promises, faith is an unavoidably personal reality. Faith is not something we can skip over since it makes constant demands on the religious person. In other words, because God confronts each of us personally, each of us has to respond to that encounter. As we will see later, I think this faith is best understood within the context of a living

Christian community, but for now we need to hear Kierkegaard's call to a personal trust in God.

Concerned that there were plenty in Denmark who imagined they had progressed beyond the gospel, Kierkegaard reminds his readers that "no one goes further" than faith. Kierkegaard describes the Christian life as the activity of faith, even in its passivity: "The person who has come to faith (whether he is extraordinarily gifted or plain and simple does not matter) does not come to a standstill in faith."[3] He compares faith to love, which cannot be spoken of in static terms, since it constantly moves upon us and touches us in our entirety. The person of faith, like the person in love, "does not go further, does not go on to something else," for to move on to something else beyond faith [or love] would be to move from the reality of faith to an "explanation" of it.[4] Faith isn't a static point of development, such as an initial acceptance of a set of assertions about God, but a mode of living, perceiving, and responding to the realities behind those assertions. The goal is not to move beyond faith but *to live by faith*.

This takes us back to the Reformation and Martin Luther, who inspired Kierkegaard, and who will also serve as our main interlocutor for the rest of this chapter.[5] In addition to expounding the doctrine of justification by faith alone, Luther also described faith as the manner of existence for the Christian. He had an admirable sense of the complexities of the human experience. Luther's use of the language "sanctification" and "sanctified" usually addresses the definitive rather than progressive nature of sanctification: the justified are the sanctified.[6] Consequently, God's elect are both justified by faith alone and also sanctified. He never downplayed the significance of faith for the Christian, since sanctification grows out of faith and is always seen as a work of God's grace. This is what Kierkegaard was saying, in his own way, centuries later.

Luther's emphasis on faith also shaped his view of the Christian's struggle with sickness.[7] With the loss of health, a person—whether in the sixteenth century or the third millennium—commonly loses a sense of peace and identity; physical difficulties are often accompanied by spiritual trials, even though tracing out the exact relationship between the two is impossible. A person's life becomes severely limited by debilitating pain or weakness. Amid such difficult seasons of life, Luther understood that the fog of doubt often obscures the believer's vision: accordingly, the taunts of hell often grow louder during those periods. He recognized this because he lived it himself.

Sometimes Luther experienced such severe physical ailments that he thought he was on the verge of death,[8] frightening not only his wife and friends but even himself.[9] He was anything but stoic at these times; given that he viewed physical pain as often woven together with spiritual challenge, he approached such moments like a sailor fighting a vicious storm that would inevitably leave damage and pain. Amid such storms he believed "all hands on deck" were needed to survive the turbulence.[10]

For example, in 1527 he wrote to Melanchthon, explaining how for a full week he was terribly ill and "in death and hell." He wrote, "I almost lost Christ in the waves and blasts of despair and blasphemy against God, but God was moved by the prayers of saints and began to take pity on me and rescued my soul from the lowest hell."[11] Luther knew that in times of physical and emotional distress saints often struggle to believe and are afflicted with confused images of God and his work in the world. During such seasons the Christian leans heavily on the faith and prayers of other saints, for by them one is sustained or even "rescued."

Writing to Nicholas Hausmann on another occasion Luther described how he stood in the midst of great suffering even as the plague seemed to be ending in his area: at least three times the affliction had hit his household, with even his own son Hans greatly malnourished and ill, appearing for a time to be on the verge of death.[12] In this case the sickness was not his own but that of those he loved, and so again he admits that while it is "Christ's will," he has still been struggling with "restlessness and faintheartedness." Consequently he implores Hausmann for prayers that "my faith fail not."[13] Luther never doubted the significance of faith, but he also never forgot how fragile it could become under stress. What was really at stake then was not merely his physical condition but his belief in God's goodness and provision.

While Luther's life was marked by various battles, including struggles against the pope and other power structures, he always seemed to have a sense that his underlying battle was one of faith. As David C. Steinmetz concludes, "The central problem for Luther remains the problem of God. The mercy and compassion of God are always set against the background of God's hiddenness."[14] Luther repeatedly wrestled with the questions, Is God really loving? Could he welcome a sinner like Luther into his holy presence? Would Luther's heart worship this God or merely fear him?

Luther lived, as Heiko Oberman said, between "God and the devil," and so he serves as a useful model of the Christian struggle.[15] When he suffered from serious sickness, the threefold taunt of sin, death, and the devil was always nearby. Original sin brought judgment and brokenness into this world, including illness. The ache of disease often awakens an awareness of one's sin, thus increasing even the believer's susceptibility to imagine divine judgment. Those living with such pain are often made more aware of the darkness of death, a darkness that allows the devil to move about like a lion, seeking to devour the vulnerable. I will address this more fully in chapter ten. At stake during these times of illness is the saint's ability to trust in God's gracious reign and rule. What is needed is light, the light of faith.[16]

Illness was unquestionably tangled up with spiritual trial in Luther's mind. And, as the editors of the classic collection of Luther's correspondence put it, his afflictions were often accompanied with "spiritual depression."[17] Justus Joan wrote as a firsthand witness of a time when Luther was suddenly overcome with serious physical pains after having gone through a "grave spiritual trial" earlier in the morning.[18] That evening Luther's body gave out, starting with ringing in his ear but then quickly spreading so that his entire flesh seized up until he appeared frighteningly faint. Luther's response was not only to beg Justus to splash him quickly with cool water, but he also began to pray fervently. His prayers in this instance, as we have them recorded by Justus, are a mixture of his reciting the Lord's Prayer and various psalms. Luther was mainly just physically weak, and so his friends brought physical relief, but just as important to his mind was their encouragement and comfort. They reminded him of his hope, which we will talk about more. Turning to everyone in the room one by one, Luther requested, "Pray for me, please."[19] Thinking he was about to die, Luther alternated between giving what appear to be final encouragements to Katie, his wife, and fits of prayer. But Luther did not die, and when the physical pains subsided and he was more stable the next day, he reported that he had just been to "school" and that "his spiritual trial of yesterday was twice as great as this bodily illness which came on in the evening."[20] While it may be debated whether spiritual trials provoke physical vulnerability, or how bodily weakness may open one up to spiritual challenges, these two struggles often go together for us just as they did for Luther.

Writing to Gerard Wilskap at Herford in 1528, Luther noted that while he had suffered illness from his youth, he was now facing things at their most severe. "So far Christ has triumphed," he wrote, "but He holds me by a very slender thread," and so Luther desperately requests their prayers: "I have saved others, myself I cannot save."[21] Luther wants to be "saved" not merely from death but more importantly from blasphemy, doubt, and distrust of his loving God. Asking for others to petition God on his behalf, he recognizes the paradox that such prayers are offered for "dead men who live, as captives who are free, as sufferers who are safe."[22] God employs his people's prayers to help the saints genuinely feel alive, free, and safe, even as they at times are tempted to believe they are dead, enslaved, and insecure. Luther recognized not only the centrality of faith but also the dependence we have on others through their prayers and presence to provide a hedge around us during our weakness.[23]

God freely employs the faith of others, expressing itself through prayer, to sustain and uphold the faith of the suffering Christian. Faith is not simply the means through which a person becomes a Christian but also the essential manner of the Christian life. The wounded believer often depends on other saints to sustain them through seasons of suffering. While Luther and others from the Reformation are often accused of brash individualism in their conceptions of faith, these records of Luther's sickness remind us that he never imagined faith as a purely individual activity. Yes, the individual was called to believe, but that faith can in fact only be lived within an organic connection to the locally constituted church. One of the regular ways the body of Christ maintains its health, even as parts of the body are attacked with disease, is for the other parts to carry some extra weight. When a person's ankle is broken, they instinctively place more weight on the strong leg. This is not because they despise the weak leg but because it can only return to full health if its burden is borne by the other limb. Similarly, Christians bear one another's burdens (cf. Gal 6:1-5).

These insights from the Scriptures and from Luther and Kierkegaard push us to conclude that our responses to suffering must include giving attention to the physical, social, and psychological needs of the wounded saint as well as offering the faith, prayers, and acts of mercy of the surrounding body of Christ to the distressed pilgrim (cf. 2 Cor 1:4-7). Thus in our own distress, when we find it easy to doubt God's grace and provision, the body of Christ gives shelter and sustenance under the canopy of their faith. As the body of Christ we can together face any worries about divine apathy, judgment, or abandonment. The flame of individual faith weakens when it is alone, but in true community the fire of faith illumines the night.

HOPE

> Why are you cast down, O my soul,
>> and why are you in turmoil within me?
> Hope in God; for I shall again praise him,
>> my salvation and my God. (Ps 42:5-6)

> My Lord God, give me once more the courage to hope;
> merciful God, let me hope once again,
> fructify my barren and infertile mind. (Søren Kierkegaard)[24]

Christian faith does not simply involve affirming God's existence but the far more difficult call to trust in God's holy kindness and tender provision. John Calvin described faith as "a firm and certain knowledge of God's benevolence toward us, founded upon the truth of the freely given promise in Christ, both revealed to our minds and sealed upon our hearts through the Holy Spirit."[25] Maintaining a "firm and certain knowledge" can sound easy when things are going well, but the pain, misery, injustice, despair, and hypocrisy in the world assault our confidence in any good and gracious God. Prolonged physical suffering easily induces despair and fatigue, both for the sick and for the caregivers. Hope, which nourishes faith, thus plays a pivotal role in sanctification.

Seasons of physical distress challenge Christian hope, so the suffering saint leans hard upon other believers for spiritual sustenance. Fellow pilgrims strengthen us by embodying gospel promises. Notice that Calvin's definition of faith doesn't ground confidence in the Lord's benevolence by making empirical observations about the way the world works (which in fact is full of injustice and pain); instead, his certainty is "founded upon" the realities of the Son and Spirit. And the promises of Christ and the power of his Spirit are normally linked to the people of God.

Under the previous heading of "faith," we noted that the saints *speak to God for us* when we struggle to believe and speak alone. Further, the saints are also called to *speak to us for God* when we seem unable to hear him on our own. Their prayers sustain our faith; their proclamation reignites our hope. Hope is not achieved through the power of positive thinking but in receiving the promises of the Word and sacraments. Of course, one can read the Scriptures while alone, and the individual must swallow the bread and wine, but the corporate life of the church strengthens the soul by reminding us that we are not alone but in a body. Here our particularity and community meet.

The Holy Spirit mysteriously draws us into communion with God in the administration of the sacraments and the proclamation of the Word. For example, the psalms often display a movement from anxiety to hope.[26] Beginning occasionally with a sense of abandonment or peril, the psalms urge the singer or reader to invoke the power of remembrance and anticipation. Remember who this God is, the Creator Lord who has been faithful through the ages. Remember the stories of his deliverance, his constant care, his steadfast love. Such remembrances rekindle hope by assuring the sufferer that Yahweh neither leaves nor forsakes us. They offer comfort to those who suffer, whether their pain comes as a result of national exile or physical weakness. Offering generation after generation a hymnbook to shape their memory of God's trustworthiness, the corporately sung and recited psalms have renewed the hope of his people without denying the struggle of living in a fallen world. These songs affirm the pain and perplexity of life, but they call us to trust God even during these seasons. Significantly, the psalms do not attempt to explain suffering or what mysterious purposes God may have for our pain. Instead, they display the character of Yahweh as trustworthy, brimming with compassion for his people. In this movement from despair to hope, the wounded saint is not belittled, as some like Dorothee Soelle fear, but rather reminded of our Redeemer's fatherly concern that still mysteriously moves in and through his compromised creation that so longs for shalom.[27]

Returning to Luther for a moment, we observe that in his "Preface to the Psalms" he wrote of their value compared to the popular books of his day on the legends of the saints. Luther observed that such stories, depicting the glorified lives of the saints, never had the saints speak, for their "tongues were tied."[28] For Luther, human speech is a vital aspect of what separates us from the animals. In this way the psalms resonate with us because "every man on every occasion" can easily find words in the psalms that speak to their struggle. Here we can find words to speak when we become speechless. Or, to put it differently, the community can speak or sing these sacred words when it does not know what to say. Luther observes that the romanticized lives of the saints promote the "beginnings of sects and factions" so that they tend to "lead and even drag one away from the fellowship of the saints."[29] The beauty of the psalms is that they openly move from the depths of despair to the glories of hope: they neither belittle pain nor trivialize promise. In the psalms the church is "depicted in living colours," able to encourage the saint, comfort the afflicted, and humble the proud.[30] It makes sense, then, that upon hearing of his father's death, after much weeping and anguish, Luther turned to his psalter.[31]

The psalms not only give us voice with which to pray to God, but in them we also hear God's voice to his people. They show us that we can trust the Creator to handle the details of creation, including the lives of his people (e.g., Ps 8; 93; 104; 148); he is the Shepherd who cares for his sheep even as they walk through the valley of darkness (e.g., Ps 23; 28; 80). He is the Lord who governs with wisdom and love (e.g., Ps 5; 25; 36; 86; 89; 136), the God of his people who will not forget them in their time of need (Ps 94), and the one who is worthy to be praised even amid our trials (Ps 95). By retelling the stories of God's acts of deliverance and concern, the psalms renew the hope of God's people.

Similarly, the epistle to the Hebrews functions like an extended sermon given to a struggling congregation.[32] Relying heavily on the testimony of the Old Testament, it contains one of the most extended discussions of faith found in the Bible and describes faith being nurtured in hope. Hebrews 11 walks us through the history of God's people, moving from Abraham to the intertestamental period. The chapter provides great examples of personal faith, always presenting that faith in light of God's faithfulness. Hebrews 10:23 tells us, "Let us hold fast the confession of our hope without wavering, for he who promised is faithful." The saints' examples of faith provide the means by which God's faithfulness is revealed. In chapter 11 the author calls the congregation to put their hope in the God who has been faithful to the saints who have gone before them. Whether one thinks of Noah, Sarah, Jacob or "the women [who] received back their dead by resurrection" (Heb 11:35), their faith was upheld by the steadfastness of divine character and promises. Again, like the psalms, it does not offer hope through denial or escape but by looking at the way God has delivered the saints in the past and at the eschatological promises for the future. These saints kept their hope in Yahweh despite their deep distress, their physical weakness, and the threat of death. "Hope" is used throughout Hebrews, concludes William Lane, as a "vivid reminder that the entire Christian life is christologically and eschatologically stamped."[33] All of these stories point to the promised Messiah who has come, who suffered as our high priest on behalf of his people, who has secured our future even amid the apparent insecurity of our present (Heb 6:20), for he now sits at the right hand of God (Heb 10:12). Through the Word proclaimed, the people of God found their hope in the crucified, risen, and ascended Christ.

Our hope, then, grows out of a confidence in God's redemptive actions and trustworthy presence. Further, we don't have to rely on ourselves to muster this hope when we are physically or mentally vulnerable, because God gives us others to bring this proclamation, to sing these songs to us. Our fellow saints speak to us for God. They remind us that God never forgets his people, for this is the God and Father of Jesus Christ, who offers a foretaste of what is to come when he heals the sick and provides for the needy. Because Jesus Christ is the hope of the gospel, God's people proclaim to each other the good news of Christ crucified and risen. In our weakness we may find it impossible to proclaim this hope ourselves, but when it is given to us in the liturgy or by fellow pilgrims, when we hear "Christ is risen," we are able to reply, "He is risen indeed!"

LOVE

> There is no fear in love, but perfect love casts out fear. (1 Jn 4:18)

To the sufferer, the body of Christ offers faith and graciously supplies needed gospel hope. Yet by the remark in 1 Corinthians 13 that of these three—faith, hope, and love—the greatest of these is love, Paul shapes our understanding of them and how they affect each other.

Even great gifts can be upended and used for ill. Faith without love can turn abusive, belittling the struggling saint by substituting impersonal axioms for heartfelt prayers. Likewise, hope void of love can devolve into insensitive forms of activism and arrogance, replacing empathetic grace with cheap platitudes or an impersonal vision of what must be done. So if faith and hope are to mean anything to us in our suffering, they must come to us in the context of love, or, to put it another way, faith and hope are only properly applied with love: a love accomplished and given through the person and work of Christ.

Love is what we are called to, and love is what we should never try to escape from. But in this fallen world, such love also brings with it real suffering. Nicholas Wolterstorff, grieving over the death of his son, writes,

> Suffering is a mystery as deep as any in our existence. It is not of course a mystery whose reality some doubt. Suffering keeps its face hid from each while making itself known to all. . . . We are one in suffering. Some are wealthy, some bright; some athletic, some admired. But we all suffer. For we all prize and love; and in this present existence of ours, prizing and loving yield suffering. Love in our world is suffering love. . . . This, said Jesus, is the command of the Holy One: "You shall love your neighbor as yourself." In commanding us to love, God invites us to suffer.[34]

We experience divine love most concretely when we receive and give it to others. God expresses his love and extends his comfort through his people. This expresses not merely a sociological observation but a theological analysis of the relational nature of God's being and work.

One aspect of our union in Christ is our union with one another. The church, as the body of Christ, has "no division in the body, but . . . the members . . . have the same care for one another" (1 Cor 12:25). Our union with Christ, and therefore with each other, is based on and powered by his love for us, which flows through us to each other and to the world around us. We see the tender side of this love in St. Paul's remark that "if one member suffers, all suffer together, if one member is honored, all rejoice together" (1 Cor 12:26). Similarly, the faith of all strengthens the faith of each. The weakened hope of one receives hope from the ministry of the others. Faith and hope thus receive their essential character, power, and efficacy from the love that unites the whole body. When faith and hope grow out of love, they are like food for the hungry and medicine for the sick. Thus we need faith, hope, and love, but without love we lose all three.

Luther helps us here too. He demonstrates the relationship between suffering and sanctification as it works out within the context of the community, even in its imperfect expressions of love. Eric W. Gritsch explains that when unpacking his view of communion of the saints as his definition of the church, Luther emphasized the role of the Holy Spirit in calling the saints together in fellowship.

> Accordingly, the church consists of people who are incorporated into Christ and each other like the ingredients of a cake: none is for himself, but instead each is blended with the others in the fellowship of love. Luther himself depended on the "consolation of the brethren" (*consolatio fratrum*) whenever he suffered inner turmoil and temptation—especially in the year 1527, when he was plagued by illness, the loss of friends, and various other forms of *Anfechtung*. Communion meant true communication to Luther, through word and sacrament, in the giving of oneself to Christ and to one's neighbor. Just as Christ emptied himself for the world on the cross (Phil. 2:5-11), so the Christian is to empty himself to his neighbor in love.[35]

Luther was clearly not naive about the turbulence of living among sinful saints, and so perfectionist portraits of the church did not seduce him. Yet he never let cynicism crowd out his theological instincts that the healing power of communion with God is found in the prayers, words, and love of the saints. For as the body of Christ, the saints are connected to one another and to their Head, so that Luther can confidently conclude, "When we feel pain, when we suffer, when we die, let us turn to this, firmly believing and certain that it is not we alone, but Christ and the church who are in pain and suffering and dying with us."[36] Within the matrix of love, Luther holds the church and the Savior together through a robust view of union with Christ.

And yet vital as our fellow pilgrims are as a means to our sanctification amid suffering, we ultimately look not to them but *with them* to the revelation of God in Christ. For faith, hope, and love all must ultimately point to and come from the triune God and not merely from the community of the saints. This is why we can never stop returning to the key Christological images: incarnation, cross, and resurrection.

10

CONFESSION AND THE OTHER

It is in the shelter of each other that the people live.

Irish Proverb

Confess your sins to one another and pray for one another,
that you may be healed.

James 5:16

"Suffering is feeling the weight of this broken world," said Josh. Suffering, for Josh, was not a philosophical debate but the shared pain of his chronically ill wife and his dying father. Josh was the caretaker rather than the one who felt the pain directly, and his presence in their lives was a grace. But each of these three needed pastoral care.

Annie faced cancer as a young woman. Going through chemotherapy, she can tell you exactly how many times she was mistaken for a boy (twenty-seven!). The emotional and physical scars she endured took her to some dark places, but they also opened up opportunities for light, grace, and hope. In all this, she needed others to sustain her in the pilgrimage of faith.

Samantha has dealt with chronic pain since she was young. Now a grandmother, she has always experienced unceasing discomfort. She says, "I am constantly hurting." Now diagnosed with fibromyalgia, she often had the feeling that no one acknowledged her pain; some of the early doctors simply responded with snide comments rather than acceptance. Her physical pain was not obvious to the onlooker, which made it difficult for others to recognize, affirm, and come alongside her when she needed it most. So she became suspicious of others and also of herself.

Through the years of research, counseling, and teaching, I have heard countless stories. This is but a taste of them. While names and identifying features are normally changed, these narratives and others throughout this book grow out of those conversations I have been honored to have as people would entrust their stories to me. They are all real stories of real people with real pain. However, if you are reading this book, the odds are you could easily add plenty of other stories, with different names, symptoms, and challenges. What unifies the stories is the suffering.

Because of our family's experience, I have a particular concern for those who face daily pain. A fairly accepted definition of chronic pain is physical suffering that lasts more than three months. In other words, if you woke up to intense pain everyday for the past ninety days, you will likely wake up on day ninety-one no longer surprised by your physical distress. That doesn't ease the discomfort, of course; it just means that it has become your new normal, your new reality. And with that new norm, all manner of challenges arise, from muscular atrophy to unwelcome bouts of depression.

For some, when the pain is intense, a person just wants to be left alone, but being alone is often not a safe place to be. Serious physical pain often exposes us to the torrential acid rains of frustration, self-condemnation, and despair; these add a spiritual and emotional dimension to physical suffering that was already almost unbearable. It should not be surprising that those who suffer chronic pain are thus at a greater risk of suicide than the general population.[1] Clearly the physical pain is not the only problem here.

We are multidimensional creatures: when our bodies hurt, we also suffer in our intellect, our emotions, our will, and our souls.[2] And I have become convinced that those—and here I am especially thinking of Christians—who face intense physical pain often also struggle with feeling judged.

PAIN AND PUNISHMENT?

Those unfamiliar with prolonged physical suffering may be surprised to learn that chronic pain exposes people to the fear they are being punished. But those who have lived an extended time with pain will probably not be shocked to learn that the term *pain* comes, etymologically (historically), from the Latin *poena*, which means "punishment," "penalty," or "retribution."[3] We have a shared, centuries-long emotional impulse to link pain with punishment. The more I watch, listen, ask, and research, the more convinced I am that it is a common Christian experience to feel that our personal pain is a sign of condemnation.

I remember speaking with a godly couple who had experienced a heart-rending miscarriage—and not their first. Here were some of the most godly people I have ever known, and yet they feared that this had happened because of some sin of theirs. They kept probing their lives for some explanation. Do you know what any of us find when we engage that level of introspection? We find sin. We discover pride, jealousy, anger, and who knows what else. These were two of the most faithful Christians I can imagine, yet they were asking if this suffering was the result of their sin. Well, the truth is that they were and are both sinners. Any of us who examines our lives carefully enough will discover this—and it can be far more frightening than we want to admit. Thus they experienced this pain as a personal punishment.

Yet it is not simply the sufferer who is prone to make such connections. In subtle but significant ways, outsiders also communicate that the person's suffering is a result of sin. So, while we are uncomfortable actually saying, "You are suffering physical pain because of your sin," that is often the impression we give to the sufferer, whether that was our intention or not.

Sometimes these accusations come directly, such as when people let you know that they believe you must have done something thus far undiscovered (e.g., lied, cheated, were slothful), and therefore you are now enduring this pain because of your sins (cf. Job's friends). On the other hand, in our culture these accusations are often more subtle and indirect, but that doesn't make them any less hurtful. As a correlate of our culture's success and obsession with health, we sometimes speak of illness as the sufferer's own fault: Jim is really in physical pain because he has not avoided gluten. Nicole wouldn't have faced breast cancer if she had only breast-fed her children longer, or

Stan could have avoided the heart attack if he had only taken a small aspirin everyday, or . . .

We don't normally say these things to people's faces, but everyone can sense the judgments, the accusations, and the tension. The dots are clearly there to be connected: physical pain comes as a consequence of personal shortcomings and therefore sin. It is their just punishment.

Culturally we may have moved away from using the language of punishment because we find it offensive. But in actual experience those who endure chronic pain still very much see it as retribution. Our culture generates these accusations from within and from without, sometimes pronounced, but far more often subtly, even in a passive-aggressive manner from those nearby.

So what are we to do? It is tempting at this point to simply dismiss *sin* from this discussion. We are rightly tempted to conclude, "That is absurd, people are just feeling physically devastated, so we shouldn't be talking about their sin at all; we should be talking about getting their bodies healthy." I completely understand this sentiment, since it reflects a heart of compassion and a better theology than reductive retribution. And by all means it is not wrong to talk about possible ways to improve their health. Yet because discussions of sin can so easily go sideways when dealing with people in pain, we are tempted to go to the other extreme, leaving it altogether out of the equation. Unfortunately, our fear of hurting people in this way can leave us less than fully helpful to the sufferer.

While we should reject the idea of simplistic retribution, we should not miss the fact that sin is a real problem. And it is a real problem even for those in chronic pain. Simply facing pain everyday does not free us from sin. Nor does it make us more sinful. But what it does tend to do is *heighten our awareness of sin and brokenness in the world and in our own life.* In a counter-intuitive way, those who are hurting can also help those who are relatively free from pain: they remind us that the world—including our body—is not as it should be, and suffering and the pains of death never let us forget this. But with these sisters and brothers we can also see the promise of shalom and hope, a promise not yet fully realized. To understand these dynamics we must learn why those who suffer often have a heightened awareness of the reality of sin, not only in themselves but in the world.

PAIN AND ACKNOWLEDGING OUR SIN

There are good reasons for Christians to avoid trying to interpret physical pain as punishment from God.[4] And yet people who suffer physically often also have an increased awareness of their sin. This is where things get tricky. I am most definitely not saying that those who suffer are more sinful than others. Jesus warns against such simplistic equations (Lk 13:4-5). But those who face deep or extended pain sometimes have a heightened awareness of their own sin and even of the brokenness of our world. Let me explain what I mean.

People speak of the "terrible twos," when a child stereotypically thinks only "me, me, me," throwing fits and creating mayhem when they don't get their way. Now is that two-year-old a greater sinner than a forty-year-old who doesn't throw toys across a room and never raises their voice at others? Or might it be that the heart of a forty-year-old and that of a two-year-old are indeed similar, as we all struggle with the desire to be the center of attention and to get what we want? One of the big differences between the two-year-old and the forty-year-old is that the latter has a greater mastery of social expectations and etiquette. In other words, the forty-year-old just knows how to hide sin more effectively than the two-year-old.

Similarly, the elderly, as they lose their strength—physically, emotionally, and mentally—can sometimes be more prone to words and actions that earlier in their lives would never have come out. There was a family whose deeply loved and respected matriarch went into her last years with so much physical suffering that she became very difficult to be with, saying and doing some things that were very hurtful. But in truth, most of us have such proclivities, but we are able to exercise some level of control over letting our internal world be seen by those on the outside.

Here is the interesting point: our ability to hide our sin gets compromised when we are exhausted and in constant pain. It becomes much more difficult to pretend that we are fine.

What if you, like a woman I know, face every waking moment with a headache? Not a normal headache like many of us experience from time to time, but as she described it, the "I want to rip my head off" or "kill myself" kind of headache. There were times when she would have to lock herself in her bathroom to get away from light, since it was the only room in the apartment without a window. And then she would try to cover the cracks under the door with towels to make sure no other light got in. Lying on the floor, she would just weep and feel the pain. Such a person is very vulnerable, not merely to the despair of physical hurt but also to wild self-accusations. Luther, locked in a room alone with himself, often felt that the only other person in the room was the devil; the accuser would bring charges against Luther, flood him with memories and regrets, sometimes with things that were true and sometimes with things that were not true. The accusations hurt, adding to an already miserable situation. Pain suffered in isolation does not make a person more of a sinner, but it does tend to remove our defenses against accusations and lingering sorrows.

A physically healthy person has both a properly functioning body and more energy and ability to "keep it together." Not only can we present ourselves to the world as good and upstanding, but we can also easily convince ourselves that we don't really have any big sin problems. We ignore our offenses, hiding them both from others and from ourselves. However, when chronic pain or intense suffering comes on us, our resilience and energy desert us, leaving us wilted and limp. We see parts of our lives and our hearts that we desperately wish were not there. Our isolation removes the support of others and makes us vulnerable to depression and other types of darkness. What are we to do?

THE VALUE AND LIMITS OF PREACHING TO YOURSELF

What are you to do when you, as a Christian, are struggling with pain and depression? What are you to do when you feel the weight of your sin sitting on you like a heavy piece of concrete, threatening your ability to breathe, to think, to live?

One response that has become fairly popular in recent decades is the idea of "preaching the gospel to yourself." I believe this approach is helpful but usually insufficient. D. Martyn Lloyd-Jones made this idea popular in his opening reflections in *Spiritual Depression*. Lloyd-Jones observes that when depression sets in, we are *listening* rather than *talking* to ourselves: "We allow our self to talk to us instead of talking to our self."[5] He rightly observes how easy it is to lambast ourselves, listening to internal accusations, focusing on the negative, and seeing only our sin. This internal voice brings a wave of condemnation, fear, and frustration (cf. 1 Jn 3:20).

As a response, Lloyd-Jones encourages us to follow the example of the psalmist who speaks to himself boldly and emphatically: "Why are you cast down, O my soul, and why are you in turmoil within me?" (Ps 43:5). Instead of *listening* to his soul, he then *speaks* to it: "Hope in God; for I shall again praise him, my salvation and my God." Then, as the psalm continues, he reminds himself of God's character and promises. This example calls us to speak what is true to ourselves and to receive thereby comfort and courage from God. This focuses our minds and hearts on who God is, what he has done, and how the gospel is actually good news. Embrace these realities and let them become more determinative for shaping our mental landscape rather than the depression that lingers. And he further advises us to take up a level of what he calls defiance: "Defy yourself, and defy other people, and defy the devil and the whole world, and say with this man: 'I shall yet praise Him for the help of His countenance, who is also the health of my countenance and my God.'"[6]

There is much wisdom here. Augustine, Luther, and Wesley similarly counseled their followers to preach to themselves and embrace the good news of Jesus and his kingdom. Still, the weakness of this prescription, taken by itself, is that it is overly individualistic, ignoring our nature as members of a larger body, and thus also inherently unstable when isolated. Lloyd-Jones's assertion that "the main art in the matter of spiritual living is to know how to handle yourself" ignores the problem that we don't always know how to handle ourselves, nor can we be trusted to handle ourselves. We need others. Of course, at his best Lloyd-Jones knew this. That is partly why he believed so strongly in the value of preaching. But here I would like to examine neither self-talk nor public preaching but the Christian act of confession. For here is a classic Christian conception on what to do when we are struggling with sins and condemnation threatens to set in upon us. We have evidence of early believers practicing mutual and sometimes public confession.[7] And while Protestants most often associate confession with the Roman Catholic tradition, it has always been a biblical call and practice throughout the ages.[8] Protestants must be careful not to throw the baby out with the bathwater.

I believe the act of confession, and in particular confession to a fellow believer, is crucial to sustaining the struggling saint. As we will soon see, for those facing physical suffering—where they have a heightened sense of their own sin—this act of confession becomes one of the keys to life-giving faith amid the voices of condemnation. This is not because they are greater sinners but because they sometimes have a greater sensitivity to the presence of sin in their lives and this world, and they sense their deep need for forgiveness and grace. We all need these gifts of divine compassion and mercy, but our relative health often masks the darker realities of our spiritual neediness.

CONFESSION OF SIN AND OUR NEED FOR FELLOW BELIEVERS

God calls us to live in the real world, not in some imaginary world of wishes and ideals. Confession of sin is a reckoning with that real world, a reckoning with ourselves before God. It is an opportunity to set our lives back into the comfort and affection of our heavenly Father, who forgives our sins, cleans us up, heals our wounds, and strengthens us to go out again into the everyday. Further, since we are not simply individuals but members of a body, it is worth asking how confession relates to that community and what it might look like in that setting.

The following comments will draw heavily from Dietrich Bonhoeffer's discussion in his volume *Life Together* (1938).[9] Germany in the late 1930s was a context of intense pressure, where the external struggles of the moment made it easy to avoid discussions of personal sin and confession, concentrating instead on political and social evils. Although Bonhoeffer shows his awareness of such collective evils, and his commitment to resisting them is well documented, he finds nonetheless that confession is still an important part of the Christian's life. He seeks to answer three questions in particular that pertain to the discussion in this book:

- Why are others helpful for confession?
- Who is qualified to hear confessions?
- What does such confession do?

Why are others helpful for confession? Why do we find it easier to admit our sins to God than to another Christian? We might suspect that the reverse would be true, since God is holy, just, and all-knowing, while fellow believers are sinners like us. Bonhoeffer suggests that the former is easier because we have been "deluding ourselves about our confession of sin to

God."[10] That is, we have not actually confessed our sins to God at all, but we have instead been "confessing our sins to ourselves and also forgiving ourselves."[11] Consequently, we can sometimes sense that this is what we are doing, so we wonder if we really are forgiven. This produces a harmful cynicism, since we imagine we will let ourselves off too easily.

Christian confession does not just require sympathy; it requires honesty. Private confessing to God alone can thus deny us a sense of forgiveness if we doubt our own honesty with God. This is where our fellow believers and friends can help as they help break what Bonhoeffer calls the "circle of self-deception."[12]

We break our isolation when we confess our sins before another Christian. Our brothers and sisters in Christ are the means of a grace that I cannot channel to myself, namely, the physical presence of someone who is not me. I cannot control or distract them the way I can do to myself.

The goal of this action is not that they will say, "Oh, don't worry, it isn't that bad" or "That is not that big of a deal, everyone thinks that . . ." The goal, as stated earlier, is to reckon with reality, and that requires honestly facing the truth. Otherwise the exercise is useless. This makes confession of concrete sins to others difficult, because we all fear the vulnerability to others that must accompany the naming of specific sins. To be forgiven, healed, cleansed, and restored to God requires that our offenses, diseases, dirt, and alienation be obliterated and that we experience the consequent forgiveness, healing, cleansing, and restoration. This requires an honest reckoning. Confession before others, therefore, to be of any use at all, requires that those others are safe and trustworthy and that we are open with them. Normally, those who receive our confessions must have enough life and spiritual experiences in line with what is confessed to serve us well. Later I will say more on qualifications for hearing confession.

Bonhoeffer understood how incredibly difficult it is for us to confess sin before another who knows us and who will be around in the future. To be specific is far too painful for most of us, but Bonhoeffer encourages us to be specific rather than vague. God forgives our sins—not just sin in general but our particular sins. Still, this can be hard to believe.

The sixteenth-century Heidelberg Catechism gives Christians a tool for confessing their faith in a very personal way instead of as an abstraction. Without neglecting the doctrines of revelation, justification by faith, atonement, and so on, it prompts the Christian to confess that "not only to others, but to me also God has given the forgiveness of sins, everlasting righteousness and salvation, out of sheer grace."[13] Not just Johnny's sins are forgiven—that may be easy enough to believe. I can imagine God forgiving him. But *my* sins are forgiven. This Shepherd knows *my* name, calls me personally and specifically. He offers himself *for me*, for *my* sins, for *my* new life. These are not abstract ideas but personal facts that liberate our hearts. We need to hear the gospel from others, from outside ourselves. The power of the gospel preached personally to me from a faithful sister or brother has a power that I cannot conjure for myself.

Who is qualified to hear confessions? We must face three truths: we sin, we need forgiveness and grace, and we are not necessarily the best ones to convince ourselves that we are forgiven. The third statement by itself should remind us that at least occasionally we need to make confession of sin to others and not just privately before God.

We are not always honest with ourselves about our sin, even before God. We know this, so we don't trust ourselves. Therefore, when we declare to ourselves, "You have a sympathetic High Priest, and in him your sins are forgiven," we like the words but doubt they really apply to us personally. We are too aware of our sin, and simply repeating the words to ourselves doesn't seem to make them become more true. Further, our disbelief in our self-assurances fosters isolation rather than community. We feel the need to hide from others, and that encourages a life in darkness rather than light. How do we break this cycle? Only with the help of others.

Yet if we need others to receive our confession and to extend to us God's grace and forgiveness, where do we find these people? What qualifies them? Who, in the end, should hear our confession? Bonhoeffer's short answer is this: to be qualified, a person must be (1) a sinner, and (2) living under the cross of Christ.

Ironically, Christians sometimes act surprised when they hear about real sin. Here is where pietism becomes the enemy of faith, hope, and love, "for the pious community permits no one to be a sinner."[14] In a community that has contempt for sin, we conceal our sin and live in falsehood rather than truth. But by its very definition, being a Christian requires that we admit and not deny our sin. Hidden sins cultivate unhealthy habits and prevent genuine communion among the saints (Prov 28:13). Confession, however, heals both the individual and the community. This usually does not mean that we must confess all our sins to the whole community—there are good reasons to avoid that. As a general rule, our confession ought to be as public as our sin. For what are often deemed "private sins," it makes sense that we go to one or two others. But some sins so affect the whole community and the name of Christ that full corporate confession may be required for full restoration to take place (cf. Mt 18:15-20). Far more common, however, the whole is appropriately represented by the part: By confessing my sin to one or two in the community, and by hearing them declare the forgiveness of my sins, here I "meet the whole congregation. Community with the whole congregation is given to me in the community which I experience with this one [or two] other believer[s]."[15] Sinners are able to hear the confession of a sister or brother and proclaim forgiveness, but only if they themselves stand under the cross. Giving and receiving Christian confession of sin should be a regular part of genuine Christian friendship.

Only those who first rest themselves in the shade of the cross are in a position to offer divine grace to the confessor of sin. Here Bonhoeffer makes a distinction between the "psychologist" and the "Christian," which our great—and often appropriate—debt to psychology in our age can cause us to miss.

> The greatest psychological insight, ability, and experience cannot comprehend this one thing: what sin is. [Secular] psychological wisdom knows what need and weakness and failure are, but it does not know the ungodliness of the human being. . . . In the presence of a psychologist I am only sick; in the presence of another Christian I can be a sinner.[16]

While I greatly value the work of psychologists, Bonhoeffer's concern deserves our attention. Far too often the contemporary church has reduced its pastoral care of people to a referral to the local psychologist or counselor. Such care is important, but it cannot be the only response, as Bonhoeffer reminds us.

We need not therapy only; we need forgiveness. We need grace. And this comes to us most clearly not from those with advanced degrees but by sinners who take refuge in the shelter of the cross. "It is not experience with life but experience of the cross that makes one suited to hear confession."[17] To be under the cross is to know the depth of one's own sin. It is the great equalizer, enabling the listener not to be crushed nor horrified by whatever confession may come. The listener knows that "but for the grace of God there go I." Sinners under the cross can thus hear confession and, in the name of their Savior, extend the grace and love of God to the one in need. But only those who have experienced such grace and love themselves can truly give these gifts to others. I will say a bit more about formal confession to ordained elders, but let us not ignore this general practice of Christian friendship and love. Here is a gift we can all offer one another in the Father's love and the Son's grace, and because of our shared fellowship in the Spirit (2 Cor 13:14).

What does such confession do? We need confession because we need forgiveness, cleansing, healing, and restoration. Yet, one might respond, believers already have all this (cf. Lk 5:20; Eph 1:7; 4:32; 1 Jn 2:12). Jesus' death secures our relationship with God: it is finished (Jn 19:30; Heb 9:11-28). If we make forgiveness, cleansing, healing, and restoration contingent on the act of confession, then we risk cultivating further insecurity among God's people, for who knows if we have ever confessed all of our sins. In response, we should realize that what we are talking about here is not merely the declaration of pardon but the *experience* of pardon. What we are talking about is the Christian struggle to feel restored and to live in that restoration (cf. Mic 7:18; Col 2:12-13).

Confession before others can also help us disentangle our pain from the idea of personal punishment. Here we can know forgiveness and grace even in our pain (1 Jn 1:9). Here we can honestly affirm and confess the brokenness of the world and the failures of our own hearts. In confession, we are brought before Jesus, whom we encounter through our brother and sister (Mt 18:20; 2 Cor 2:10). Looking into their eyes, hearing their voice, and feeling their touch, we can receive Jesus's promise to us: "Your sins are forgiven."

We may not be able to take away the physical pain, but we can point one another to him who promises one day to completely heal us. For now we cling to his promise of restoration, cling to him who has the ability also to restore the body. He will make all things new (Rev 21:5). We will be free from sin, pain, and tears (Is 65:19; Rev 21:4). We will be free from isolation, self-condemnation, darkness, fear, and anger (cf. Is 35:10 // 51:11; Rev 21:22-27). We will be utterly free to love our Creator and our neighbor. While we may not fully experience that freedom now, we can help one another to experience genuine tastes of shalom even in the present, even in our pain, even as we struggle with our sin.

Confession, to be of any use, requires an often painful honesty. It takes tremendous courage and vulnerability to admit sin to another believer. "By confessing actual sins the old self dies a painful, humiliating death before the eyes of another Christian."[18] Our pride cannot handle such humiliation, which is why confession so often surprises us when it brings liberation. Even as our pride takes a massive hit, we realize we can put down our defenses for a bit and let people see who we really are and what is really true about us.

Confession liberates us not from physical pain but from shame and condemnation. And here, the "healthy" can learn from the hurting, like the blind teaching the Pharisees to see (cf. Jn 9:31–10:41). This fits with the biblical emphasis that God's people are always to be mindful of the poor, the orphan and widow, the marginalized and the neglected. Why? In part because as we are with them—as we love them and are loved by them—we are reminded that we also are poor and needy, and we rediscover the depth of God's grace to us.[19] Without others, we begin to imagine we are self-sufficient, in control, and all that we have is because of how faithful we have been. When this illusion sets upon us, we not only fail to see the truth about our need, but we also lose sight of the beauty and majesty of God.

Jesus cleansed ten lepers, but only one returned to him "when he saw that he was healed." A single man returns to Jesus and bows before him, giving thanks. Jesus' response is to wonder where the other healed lepers are. Only to this one who returns does Jesus declare, "Rise and go your way; *your faith has made you well*" (Lk 17:11-19, emphasis added). Ten were cleansed from their disease, and nine did not return to receive Christ's forgiveness, so it wasn't their faith that took away the leprosy. No, the grateful man's faith appears linked to something further, signified by being "made well." Brought before his Lord, he bows and is healed: his movement to worship rather than self-absorption brings *true healing*. Ten were cleansed, but only he was made well. Only he experienced not merely physical healing but also the grace of Christ. Only he fully heard Jesus and received the pardon of his sins. For us, meeting Jesus physically takes the form of meeting his body, the church. And so our confession, our bowing before Christ, commonly takes place in worship with his people. God's people are now the sacred place of confession, for here we meet Jesus.

MEETING CHRIST IN THE OTHER

Before I go on, I should acknowledge that Christians can and have often abused power, including hurting those who are wounded. Leaders and parishioners have been hurtful, manipulative, and insensitive. This is all undeniably true and tragic, and utterly heartbreaking. May God have mercy!

Nevertheless, as Bonhoeffer reminds us, the only way we become members of the church is by confessing ourselves to be sinners, and once we are members of this body, we do not instantly stop sinning. Instead, we start confessing. We should not let potential abuse keep us from this mercy of confession to one another. The possibility that someone will abuse our confidence should not lead us to avoid confession but to learn which people to trust and how to be a faithful hearer of others' confessions. This intimate experience brings us closer to others and enables us to experience the mercies of heaven.

By making ourselves vulnerable to others we often encounter the presence and healing of God himself (cf. Mt 18:20; 25:40, 44-45; 1 Cor 5:4; Col 3:12-17). When we are alone with our sins, we may see and feel only darkness. But with the physical presence of our fellow believer, light breaks into the darkness. No longer is sin the only thing confronting us. Now there is the other, who comes in Jesus' name to hear, receive admission of sin, and then proclaim pardon in that name which is above every name. "Those who confess their sins in the presence of another Christian know that they are no longer alone with themselves; they experience the presence of God in the reality of the other."[20] They bring to us what we may be unable to find on our own. They bring Jesus.

Through the presence of our fellow believer we receive the words, touch, embrace, and love of God. Light overcomes darkness. Through them we receive the divine benediction and the assurance that we are free from condemnation, from divine wrath, from the haunting sense that we have been abandoned or cursed by God (Rom 8:1). They help us to "hold fast our confession" of abiding in the Savior's love: "Let us hold fast our confession. For we do not have a high priest who is unable to sympathize with our weaknesses. . . . Let us then with confidence draw near to the throne of grace, that we may receive mercy and find grace to help in time of need" (Heb 4:14-16).

Our brothers and sisters reflect the Jesus of the gospel to us. He knows us, he loves us, he restores us to himself, and he calls us to live in his love no matter how weak we find ourselves. That, at its heart, is Christian obedience (1 Jn 3:23). And to live this life we need each other.

TAKE, EAT, AND DRINK

And this takes us to the Lord's Supper. Here someone else calls us to the Table and offers us the body and blood of our Savior. Someone else repeats the words of Christ, "This is my body, broken for you. . . . This is my blood, shed for you." Our confession produces not fear or embarrassment but receptivity to the grace of the Son's condescension—he came low to lift us high. He hears our confession, not to mock us or to shame us, but to liberate us in forgiveness and grace. These are the marks of his kingdom.

James writes that the elders play a special role with regard to the sick (Jas 5:14). It is worth noting that it has not always been agreed that these "elders" were necessarily the ordained clergy: Martin Luther, for example, suggested that this passage points to older and more experienced members of the congregation, but not necessarily ordained persons.[21] Calvin similarly stresses here not a sacrament of a "whispering confessional" but rather of the need for mutuality, including confession and prayer by fellow pilgrims.[22] But many if not most read the particular reference to "elders" as indicating the ordained leaders of the local congregation. These elders, chosen by the church, are the voice of the body, speaking with the authority that is theirs to the degree that they faithfully reflect the gospel. The church is called to remain true to the message of the prophets and apostles, to "bind" and "loose" by calling for repentance and extending forgiveness and grace, all in the name of Jesus (Mt 16:19; 18:18). Jesus tells his disciples, "If you forgive the sins of any, they are forgiven them; if you withhold forgiveness from any, it is withheld" (Jn 20:23). In other words, God's people are not at risk of being more just or more gracious than God himself. In Jesus' name the church, most clearly through its ordained leaders, offers the words of pardon and assurance. This is not because they themselves make God loving or kind but because they represent his divine mercy and grace. They embody the opportunity for faith, repentance, and love. They, at their best, represent divine hospitality, compassion, and life.

John tells us, "There is no fear in love, but perfect love casts out fear." Then he clarifies the fear he is talking about: it is the "fear" that "has to do with punishment" (1 Jn 4:18). Through the people of God, we are reminded that in Christ we are free from fear of divine wrath and punishment. We rest in the shadow of the cross. We are daughters and sons of the King. We can rest in his fatherly provision, care, grace, and promises. We may not experience the fullness of these divine realities this side of glory, but through the bread and wine, the community of God's people, and acts of confession and forgiveness, we gain genuine tastes of shalom. And those tastes can be the difference between life and death for all of us, but especially for those under the daily weight of physical pain.

CONCLUSION

Suffering and sin both tempt us to isolate ourselves from others. Given the reactions we often experience from others to our suffering and sin, this is not surprising. Others who will simply be with us, who know that being *with* is more important than fixing us or examining us or figuring out the whys of suffering and sin, can be hard to find. These are the ones who can hear our confession and convince us that the gospel applies to us too. These are the ones who can enable sufferers to see that their pain is no punishment. This being with is a difficult practice that displays the peace and assurance of standing in the shadow of the cross.

May we, as the people of God, care for one another in love. May we truly be the body of Christ. May we confess our sins to one another, offering honesty, grace, and transformed lives. Let us love one another in grace and truth. We are sinners. We are under the cross. Here is our hope. May it be so.

11

FAITHFUL

Suffering, like love, shatters the illusion of self-mastery. . . .
Recovering from suffering is not like recovering from disease. Many
people don't come out healed. They come out different.

DAVID BROOKS, *THE ROAD TO CHARACTER*

One of the profoundest forms of faithlessness is the unwillingness
to acknowledge our inexplicable suffering and pain.

STANLEY HAUERWAS, *NAMING THE SILENCES*

Oh come, let us worship and bow down;
let us kneel before the LORD, *our Maker!*
For he is our God,
and we are the people of his pasture,
and the sheep of his hand.

PSALM 95:6-7

In my final reflections on being faithful in the midst of suffering I
aim to be practical, offering observations with the hope that they will have
value not only for those who suffer but for the community of faith that seeks
to love them. A few key words will guide our reflections: *commitment, witness,*
compassion, particularity, mission, and *confidence.*

COMMITMENT

Pulitzer Prize–winning novelist Alison Lurie captures some of the complexity of dealing with physical pain and limitation over a long period of time. Molly, one of her characters, ruminates,

> Having a chronic illness, Molly thought, was like being invaded. Her grandmother back in Michigan used to tell about the day one of their cows got loose and wandered into the parlor, and the awful time they had getting her out. That was exactly what Molly's arthritis was like: as if some big cow had got into her house and wouldn't go away. It just sat there, taking up space in her life and making everything more difficult, mooing loudly from time to time and making cow pies, and all she could do really was edge around it and put up with it.
>
> When other people first became aware of the cow, they expressed concern and anxiety. They suggested strategies for getting the animal out of Molly's parlor: remedies and doctors and procedures, some mainstream and some New Age. They related anecdotes of friends who had removed their own cows in one way or another. But after a while they had exhausted their suggestions. Then they usually began to pretend that the cow wasn't there, and they preferred for Molly to go along with the pretense.[1]

Time after time, Christians dealing with ongoing physical pain have shared with me their experiences that unnervingly mirror Lurie's description.

Well-meaning folks start off strong, anxious to help, but not all their attempts bring benefit. For example, if you ask someone at the right time who has dealt with chronic pain—when they are feeling lighthearted—they will string together stories of the products that have been mailed to them, diets suggested, exercise regimens praised, and endless pills recommended, almost always without request or consent. Cacti juice from Arizona, intense nutritional instructions based on some obscure reading of a few verses from Genesis or Leviticus, and endless other suggestions. But, as Lurie explains, when the would-be helpers have exhausted their suggestions, their ability to continue recognizing the sufferer's pain is exhausted too. They are faced with a problem they can't alleviate, so they are ready to move on to a problem they can make disappear. And, to be honest, the sufferer is also ready to move on from the problem; unfortunately, they don't have that option. The pain is still there the next morning, as are the questions and emotional struggles. And now, added to the other problems is pressure to go along with the pretense that everything is okay. Sufferers often want to go along with the pretense as well, since they don't want to draw more attention to themselves. But this commonly contributes to their isolation; it can foster distance between what they feel internally and what those on the outside see and believe about them.

Dealing with physical pain and its complexity often means acknowledging there are no quick solutions or formulas. Frequently, what the sufferer needs most is not answers but a loving presence and lasting commitment.

Both the sufferer and those who care for them need to be committed to *faithful suffering*. They are called to be full of faith in God and faithful to one another, even amid the challenges. They are called to tell the truth about the pain and hardships even as they are faithful to point one another to Christ crucified and risen. For this to happen we need each other. It is not merely the caregiver who always upholds the wounded one. Far more often than is readily admitted, the one in pain brings courage and perseverance to the caregivers; it is most definitely not a one-way street. Each has gifts to offer and gifts to receive. This dynamic must be recognized and honored if there is going to be genuine love and care over an extended period of time. Normally this is not a short-term sprint but an exhausting marathon.

Commitment is not a popular word these days, weighed down as it is with images of unwelcome duties, drudgery, boredom, and limiting one's options. Counterintuitively, commitment often works in the opposite direction. Commitment can take the agony out of making a decision: the decision is made, so one gets on with it. And this commitment—that of a sufferer and a companion, and in some ways of the larger community—requires that they ask what faithfulness requires. It requires that all involved face facts.

The suffering is real, the lack of a solution may be an immovable fact, and the biggest truth of all is their place before God. They are held before God in Christ, the crucified and risen Lord. They are weak, and each needs to be reminded by the other of this truth. Much of the emotional anguish of suffering (as with the rest of life) comes from taking on a burden that isn't ours. The would-be helpers that Alison Lurie describes have taken on the burden of curing the pain, and they can't deal with their failure to cure it. But what is our true burden, the yoke that Christ gives us? *To love God and love each other.* This will be difficult enough without adding burdens that are not ours.

So, a true commitment of sufferer and companion(s) to each other entails a continuing investigation of God's work in *this* suffering. It will entail continuing pain, and it may last for years or a lifetime. As Eugene Peterson puts it, we are talking about a "long obedience in the same direction."[2]

WITNESS

Given the commitment described previously, how are we to respond to those who suffer? Suffering can come in many forms and be experienced in different ways: from the anguish caused by a devastating earthquake in Nepal to violence against a victim of abuse or the debilitating bodily pain that someone regularly experiences. Each case has its own distinct shape and needs its own response. But each of them brings its own real trauma. Each person will deal with it differently: some in silence, some in outbursts of rage, some with an athletic commitment to beat the grief, some with a sense of shame, and still others trying to discover a stoic detachment. What those who are trying to help do not always appreciate is that there is real power in simply walking with another person through that particular experience, bearing witness to the real challenges.

Being confused or angry or frustrated with God can actually signify an act of faith. The only people who can be really angry with God are those who actually believe he exists! Believers have often responded to pain with seeming despair without denying their Lord. Scripture is littered with the faithful—from Hannah to Jeremiah, from Ezekiel to Esther—who at some point live under the weight of suffering not apparently brought on because of personal sin.[3] For example, Naomi (in the book of Ruth) wrestles with God in her suffering and heartache, feeling the bitterness and the pain without masking it. Yet she still finds a way to hope in God's provision (Ruth 1:6), and she holds out hope that this God of mercy and grace will yet again visit her. She is, as Carolyn Custis James describes her, a female Job.[4] In this way, her apparent despair is also right next to her dogged faith, clinging to God. We should not overlook the way that faith and anguish often shape each other. Furthermore, and of crucial importance here, Naomi was not alone: Ruth walked through these tragedies with her, refusing to leave even when Naomi insisted three times that she go. Apparently Ruth received her faith from Naomi and her family (Ruth 1:4, 16-17), but now came the time for Naomi to lean on Ruth in the midst of mounting tragedies. Bound together in pain, they also were able to celebrate God's surprising provisions (Ruth 4:13-17). They point one another to God's faithfulness even amid the calamities and trials of life.

Witness holds an important place in the Christian tradition. These days when someone hears about Christian witness, they almost inevitably think about believers testifying of Christ to nonbelievers. That is what we call evangelism. However, what is often forgotten is how important giving witness or testimony can be *within* the Christian community, especially in times of difficulty.

This witness is always twofold: acknowledging that our troubles are real and that God is unflinchingly faithful. Anyone with knowledge of the history of the black church in America or personal experience in such churches recognizes the power of this practice. To this day it is common in these services to hear a speaker declare, "I need a witness," or for the congregation to respond to something being said with words of encouragement: "Testify, testify." Phrases like these normally arise when they are speaking either about the painful circumstances they are going through or about the strange and glorious ways God has met them amid their troubles. Both the pain and the provision require a witness: the voice of others helps keep you sane. "Black worship becomes an activity of nurture that bears witness to the activity of God, shows awareness and concern for life's realities, and provides nourishment in the form of communal solidarity and pastoral awareness and response."[5] Here I think predominately white Protestant churches can learn much from their sisters and brothers in the black church tradition. We must grow in our ability to hear others say, "Yes, this is really terrible," as they also encourage us that it is not merely a fantasy when we think we see God's kind hand even when there is also threatening darkness. God is with us. They see God's grace and presence too! I don't have to pick between hardship and divine concern. And so I can keep trusting God and can keep going, *but not alone.* I go with God's people rather than as a solitary individual.

Witnessing one another's pain also offers us the ability to find rest. For example, if I am really upset about something, my wife hears about it, and then she enters into my frustrations and voices similar concern, a funny thing often happens: I calm down. I don't have to keep being so angry, because now

I can see that someone else feels my pain, believes my frustration, and senses that something has gone wrong. When a friend shares my outrage I am actually quieted; I am allowed to rest, for someone else has taken up the concern. But if their response is "That is no big deal," and I am sure it actually is a big deal, then my irritation and frustrations grow rather than diminish. What I need is not for someone to tell me everything is okay; I need them to acknowledge that something is wrong—that I am not insane, but a real problem is at hand. When I see that others believe this, know this, feel this, I can calm down. I have received a witness. The witness doesn't actually make the pain go away, doesn't actually fix everything, but I no longer feel isolated; I no longer need to convince others or even myself that I am not crazy. She has said, "That is wrong" or "That seems incredibly painful." Yes and amen. Now, in the geography of our suffering, we are somewhere else, somewhere new. We have moved from an island of isolation to the mainland of community.

There are dangers here: sufferers need to beware of abusing others. If the hurt person only dumps on others and never tries to encourage them, if they only bring turmoil and never emotionally serve the other person, if they always try to achieve equilibrium at the expense of cultivating chaos in the lives of others, then there is a problem. The second half of witness is not being maintained. We must speak not just of pain but of Christ, of redemption, of hope. Nevertheless, admitting this danger does not erase the need for serving as a witness for others, and they for us.

COMPASSION

As I noted in our discussion of the emotional life of Jesus in chapter six, *compassion* is arguably the most common emotive term attributed to him. *Compassion* is to "suffer" (*pati*) "together with" (*com*) or alongside others. One way we live a cruciform life and imitate Christ is by cultivating compassion: a willingness to come alongside other people in their hurt, pain, disappointments, and even sin. It is to enter into their suffering, and by entering in, it is to take them and their suffering to the foot of the cross. Compassion also means not letting misery be the only reality. As Henri Nouwen and Walter Ganney observe in their helpful reflections on aging,

> Compassion makes us see beauty in the midst of misery, hope in the center of
> pain. It makes us discover flowers between barbed wire and a soft spot in a

frozen field. Compassion makes us notice the balding head and the decaying teeth, feel the weakening handgrip and the wrinkling skin, and sense the fading memories and slipping thoughts, not as a proof of the absurdity of life, but as a gentle reminder that "unless a wheat grain falls to the ground and dies, it remains only a single grain, but if it dies, it yields a rich harvest" (John 12:24).[6]

Our world often encourages the opposite of compassion: to view one another as competition or as a threat so that the goal is not mutual caregiving but victory, or at least detachment. Along these lines we often see and experience *schadenfreude*: this German word means "taking pleasure in the pain of another." In truth, *schadenfreude* is far more common than many of us want to admit.[7] So it takes work and the experience of grace to let compassion, rather than competition or apathy, become our orientation.

Dietrich Bonhoeffer, on the other hand, presents the idea of *stellvertretung* ("vicarious representative action"). This especially comes through in his unfinished volume, *Ethics*.[8] For him, the goal of Christian life and ethical living is not to learn and follow a set of rules but to live a life for others. To be truly human is to live for the other, on behalf of the other; in this way Jesus, in and through his vicarious life and actions, is our great representative.[9] Implications of this idea are profound when it comes to a Christian understanding of suffering.

Charles Williams, the imaginative Christian author and friend of C. S. Lewis and J. R. R. Tolkien, argued for something similar, which is commonly called "co-inherence" or the "way of exchange." As Alan Jacobs simplifies, co-inherence is "the ability of Christians, through the unifying power of the Holy Spirit that Christ had sent to his disciples, to dwell fully with each other and in one another's lives."[10] This could manifest itself by actually taking one another's pain. Though C. S. Lewis had some hesitations about this idea, he did believe that he and his wife, Joy, experienced it in 1957. She appeared to have only weeks to live, and yet all of a sudden her rapidly progressing cancer appeared to stop. He explained in a letter to Sister Penelope, "The tide began to turn—[the 'diseased spots'] were disappearing. New bone was being made. And so little by little till the woman who could hardly be moved in bed can now walk about the house and into the garden—limping and with a stick, but walking." And then, shortly after describing this in the letter, he adds, "Did I tell you I also have a bone disease?"[11] He later explained to others he believed that for a time he had received Joy's pain in his body, which partially freed her of it. Eventually her cancer reappeared and she died, but for a season Lewis thought that in some mysterious way he had entered into her pain, actually suffering with her, maybe even in her place. Similar episodes were spoken of in the early church as they cared for the sick and dying.[12]

More recently, Wheaton College president Phil Ryken has shared of his own dramatic experience of bearing another's burdens. In his 2014 convocation address, this person who rarely speaks about himself shared his story publicly.[13] Someone he loved was in bad shape, desperately low and in real trouble, facing such suffering and fear that she wondered if life was worth living. Filled with concern and love, he asked if God might remove some of her burden and place it on him. The result was that in the following weeks her burden was actually lightened more and more, but all of the sudden he began to sink into unexpected despair, filled with deep and dark thoughts. It got so bad that this man who had never doubted God's love and concern for him, never doubted his value, found himself inexplicably considering suicide. He admits that he doesn't know if there is a direct connection, but it is hard to believe there wasn't. In a most profound and mysterious way, he now suffered with—and possibly on behalf of—this loved one. Might it be that God allowed him to serve as a *Stellvertreter* or proxy for his loved one, absorbing some of her grief and pain in order that she might experience relief? He was not trying to be her messiah—that would be a misunderstanding of what was happening here or in C. S. Lewis's case: not messiah but beloved friend, deeply connected, able to be used by God to bring a season of relief to the exhausted one.

Whatever one thinks of "the way of exchange" and *stellvertretung*, the reality is that when we become committed to another Christian and walk alongside them in their suffering, we too *will* suffer. This reminds me of the proverb "Where there are no oxen, the manger is clean" (Prov 14:4). When there are no oxen, there is no manure! The only way to escape the mess of the dung is to get rid of the oxen. If one wants to escape feeling the pain of other people, there is an easy answer: Avoid all relationships! Get rid of the oxen. But then that also means you are alone, and none are there for you either. C. S. Lewis understood this when he concluded,

> To love at all is to be vulnerable. Love anything, and your heart will certainly be wrung and possibly be broken. If you want to make sure of keeping it intact, you must give your heart to no one, not even to an animal. Wrap it carefully round with hobbies and little luxuries; avoid all entanglements; lock it up safe in the casket or coffin of your selfishness. But in the casket—safe, dark, motionless, airless—it will change. It will not be broken; it will become unbreakable, impenetrable, irredeemable.[14]

We are called to have compassion, to come alongside others in their pain, and to love them. This is risky. Almost inevitably you will—even if only in some small way—suffer *with* them. However, in this shared pilgrimage you will also discover afresh the grace and tenderness of God.

PARTICULARITY

Each person, though connected to many, has their own story. And this particularity needs to be honored, but to do so requires wisdom.

I remember sitting in a hospital room alone with my sleeping wife; she had just gone through a major cancer surgery early that morning. Family and friends had given us space to rest and recover. In walked a woman I vaguely recognized, but I could not, to be honest, tell you her name. Holding fresh flowers, she came into the room and wanted to talk. Knowing what I know now, I believe she was driven to come because Tabitha's hospitalization reminded her of something she went through herself. She was not a bad person, but in truth she was not a close family friend, and I did not want to talk—especially not about how seeing Tabitha hooked up to tubes was stirring up past pains for her. She didn't mean to be hurtful, but in reality I felt somehow violated. Consequently, I have come to believe that some basic advice on relating to people facing calamities may prove helpful.

A wonderful Yiddish word is *kvetch*, which basically means "to complain." In a *Los Angeles Times* article, "How Not to Say the Wrong Thing," Susan Silk and Barry Goldman offer advice on kvetching, particularly when dealing with people who are enduring crises.[15] Since Susan faced breast cancer, they write out of the their own experience. Proposing what they call the "Ring Theory," they offer simple advice for knowing how to engage in situations like this. While almost everyone in these circumstances needs to be able both to voice complaint and receive comfort, there is a normal order to how this works.

Imagine a set of different-sized rings placed on top of one another: each larger circle is just outside of the slightly smaller circle. At the center in the smallest ring is the person in the midst of the trauma. On the far edges of the rings are mere acquaintances of the hurting person. The closer one is to the afflicted person, the closer one is to the center ring.

Simply put, it is always appropriate to offer comfort to those closer to the middle than you are, but it is only appropriate to offer complaint to those farther outside of the circle than you. The spouse of the wounded one can at times voice complaint to anyone farther outside of the center than they are, whether that be to other family members or to colleagues at work. But a distant relative cannot call up the spouse and begin to complain about how upset this situation is making them. Silk and Goldman explain, "If you want to scream or cry or complain, if you want to tell someone how shocked you are or how icky you feel, or whine about how it reminds you of all the terrible things that have happened to you lately, that's fine. It's a perfectly normal response. Just do it to someone in a bigger ring." I believe following this simple advice can greatly help us avoid unintentionally hurting people even as it also allows us to genuinely offer others our concern.

Furthermore, both those who suffer and those who attempt to care for them must be aware of the dangers of comparison. Theodore Roosevelt—or at least it is normally attributed to him—once said that "comparison is the thief of joy." A friend mentioned this comment to me, and then she went on to explain how this related to her own experience of suffering. Her relatively young father had gone into heart surgery; because of unexpected complications, he never made it out of the operating room. She was only twenty at the time, and his death was devastating. Further, hearing other people compare their experiences to hers often brought unexpected hurt. She explains,

> Christians with similar pains may have good things to say to their fellow sufferers. However, often what ends up happening is one person's suffering trumps another's, undermining the loss instead of offering true comfort.
>
> Here's a common exchange I encountered shortly after his passing:
> "I'm so sorry for your loss. Your father must have been a good man."
> "Yes sir, one of the best I will ever know."
> "If you ever wanna talk—I'm here for you."
> "Thank you, I appreciate that a lot."

"You know, my father passed away a couple years ago . . ."

And what would follow is the story of another beloved father, who passed away from cancer, old age, or perhaps a tragic accident. After those stories, a gnarling anger would well up inside me, as I compared my loss with theirs.

At least you knew ahead of time.

At least your dad saw you graduate college.

Walked you down the aisle.

At least you had the chance to say goodbye.

Unable to receive the hope another's story offered, I wept the rest of the day.

What happened there? Why did such well-meaning offerings trigger in me a nasty train of thought? They were only trying to help. Loss is excruciating at any age. Why could I not take comfort in a painful, but shared experience of losing a dad? What I discovered was that suffering isn't a contest, and comparing can often leave one person feeling guilty and the other bitter. Only when we compare our sufferings to that of Christ can we see our pain in its true light. Focusing upon the finished work of Christ delivers us from self-pity and enables us to look beyond our pain to a greater, more glorious redemptive picture.

When we encounter other's grief, it's okay to share our stories provided we connect them to the redemptive power of the gospel. I have met several women who lost their fathers at young ages and we have become a great support to one another. However, even in our very similar circumstances, we must take care to carry our sufferings to Christ. In this way we are able to comfort one another in our afflictions, sharing not just our sufferings, but also his comfort (2 Cor 1:3-5).

For some who suffer, any attempt to identity with them is welcomed. For others, any hint of comparison makes them bristle. We need wisdom to know how to navigate these turbulent waters. What is always key is honoring the particularity of a person's pain; we need to bring them, in their unique trials and tribulations, to Christ, asking that these dear ones might know, feel, and experience afresh the care and concern of their loving Lord.

MISSION

Caring for one another is a form of mission. Suffering, however, can remove all our resilience and outward attention. Every conversation gets reduced to chemotherapy updates. Every thought is consumed with fears about the future. Every ounce of energy is spent on improving one's condition. I hinted at this when we considered the role of confession in chapter ten. So how do we turn from the reactive to the proactive? Those dealing with a great deal of pain often have to work hard to avoid self-absorption and cultivate neighbor love. It takes intentionality. It takes a missional focus. But it can be life-giving.

Perhaps the main working principle of this book is realism: we continue to examine suffering as a complex reality, we examine the real effects of different kinds of interactions among people, and we look at the implications of the real salvation accomplished in Jesus Christ. Thus we reject any action that would trivialize pain or belittle the people having to deal with it. But this realism also drives us to reject any sentimentality about pain that would treat the sufferer as the center of their world. Mission, no matter how humble or relatively small, allows those in pain to look beyond their personal suffering and to experience God's grace and love as it is extended to others.

A friend of mine going through terminal cancer told me that when he was diagnosed, he and his wife knew this diagnosis necessarily meant a narrowing of their lives. Cancer would be time consuming, energy sapping, and inevitably heartbreaking. But they also knew that even for the husband's final months or years, they wanted to be committed to others. They wanted to look outside of themselves, not because they were trying to be heroic but because they knew that even while facing death the experience of neighbor love was vital to their living.

Performing small acts of care would allow them to continue to drink the fresh waters of God's love that would flow through them to others. So they simplified their commitment to three words: *hospitality, generosity*, and *curiosity*. That is being missional. They didn't want to stop being interested in other people, asking questions, hearing their stories, learning new jokes. Even with their limits, they wanted to give of themselves freely, whether that was through their finances or time or prayers. And they opened themselves to others, showing hospitality not because they had the energy to make the house look perfect or to prepare a great meal but simply for the sake of inviting others over. Sometimes guests would bring a meal or a board game or sad stories. It wasn't up to the hosts to provide everything; they just gave the space for others to experience God's peace, which surpasses understanding. This wasn't about filling a concert hall with fans but a living room with maybe two or three people. Through their questions, vulnerability, and commitment, this husband and wife were liberated from the dead end of paralyzing self-pity. And those who spent time with them in this most profound season of life testify of being cared for by two humble saints who didn't even know how significant these times became to others.

Mission will look a bit different for each of us. But what will be the same is a concern for participating in the love of God and neighbor. While sickness and suffering may change how we live, the need for love doesn't change.

CONFIDENCE

Believers are called to be confident, not in their physical stamina or in their mental abilities, nor in their clever answers, but in their merciful God. Christians are secure in the love of the Father, the grace of the Son, and in the fellowship of the Spirit. Safe in the embrace of the triune God, Christians can and do face trials and tribulations with confidence.

Even as believers grieve, lament, and wrestle amid pains and challenges, they can also experience genuine joy, love, and rest. Here Christians know there is a tension, for we do not look at tears, hurt, and grief as good things; these are the very problems God promises to one day liberate us from. And yet, this side of glory, it is also true that God can and does bring about good in the midst of the dreadful (Gen 50:20). Paradoxically, "trials of various kinds" might even be counted as a "joy," not because the difficulty is inherently good but because in the midst of it a person might taste and experience the kindness and love of God in a way that had previously been unthinkable; through this, "faith produces steadfastness" (Jas 1:2-3). How? Because we discover that God is faithful, that he never leaves us nor forsakes us. As Daniel's friends Shadrach, Meshach, and Abednego discovered, God's faithfulness does not necessarily mean we will not face the flames, but it does mean that *he* will be *with* his people in the midst of the flames (Dan 3:8-30).

The apostle Paul captures this dynamic well. Present suffering is confessed, but it is not final, and so in God's grace Christians persevere. Writing to the Corinthians he declares, "We are afflicted in every way, but not crushed; perplexed, but not driven to despair; persecuted, but not forsaken; struck down, but not destroyed; always carrying in the body the death of Jesus, so that the life of Jesus may also be manifested in our bodies" (2 Cor 4:8-10). Paul had even known an abiding physical difficulty himself, and eventually he had a vision that put things in perspective. Amid the vision, the voice of Jesus declared to him, "My grace is sufficient for you, for my power is made perfect in weakness" (2 Cor 12:9). Wrestling with his own limitations and struggle, Paul nevertheless rested in the knowledge that he experienced Christ's power in the middle of his difficulties and crises (2 Cor 11:30-31; 12:10).

The experience of a friend who lives in Australia provides a commentary on these verses. While attending seminary, Chris had a part-time job as a security guard. One morning at his job he was reading Genesis in Hebrew when, out of nowhere, a searing pain erupted behind his right eye. He told me, "It felt as if a sword had been shoved through the back of my right ocular cavity." Soon afterward a neurologist explained that he had not just experienced a migraine but a cluster headache. Remembering it as if it were yesterday, my friend could not forget the doctor's tone when he declared, "This is the third worst natural pain people can have, just after childbirth and kidney stones. I'm very sorry," he said, "but there's really nothing we can do about this." From here I will let him tell the story and give his own reflections.

> The pain repeated daily and was severe. It was not long before I simply broke down. During one of my night shifts, I realized that these headaches might never leave. When I was alone, I fell down and cried out to God. I openly cursed God. But, at that moment, I felt—almost physically—the peace of God wash over me. God overshadowed me with his presence in the midst of my rage. At that moment, I experienced the unconditional presence and grace of God.
>
> The headaches stopped soon thereafter, but it was subsequent to that time that I experienced even more significant healing. I began to actively change as a person. Everything changed: how I slept, exercised, ate, read and understood my Bible, related with my wife, and how I understood myself. According to my wife, while I was a "Christian" before, the "new changes" in me were even more significant than a "Christian conversion." I had changed as a whole person.
>
> This whole experience took on another dimension as I finished my master's thesis on Jacob's wrestling with God at the Jabbok. Since then, and like Jacob, I have by no means lived in flawless peace. However, I listen to my body much more carefully. If I overwork myself, cultivate resentment, or compete for something with too much gusto, I can feel a brief shadow pain creep into the back of my right eye once again. God does not let go of his advances! I am also thankful for this, for I know the God of Abraham, Isaac, and Jacob is the God of true peace and healing.

Cluster headaches are not a good thing, but God cares for his people even through their pain. Not everyone has such a positive experience as this brother, but what is true for all is that God never leaves his people, and he promises to never forsake them.

This brings me back to the apostle Paul. Before we can conclude with Paul's stunning promises in Romans 8, we must take a moment to recognize that he has just been quoting from Psalm 44: to fully appreciate the basis for Paul's confidence we need this context. Filled with lament and struggle, this psalm nevertheless powerfully also displays hope:

> Yet for your sake we are killed all the day long;
>> we are regarded as sheep to be slaughtered. [quoted in Rom 8:36]
> Awake! Why are you sleeping, O Lord?
>> Rouse yourself! Do not reject us forever!
> Why do you hide your face?
>> Why do you forget our affliction and oppression?
> For our soul is bowed down to the dust;
>> our belly clings to the ground.
> Rise up, come to our help!
>> Redeem us for the sake of your steadfast love! (Ps 44:22-26)

There is real pain here. The psalm begins with the struggle, claiming that the people had heard the stories: "Our fathers have told us, / what deeds you performed in their days, / in the days of old" (Ps 44:1). The problem is that the silence has been long, the pain consistent, and the clarity of God's presence and concern clouded. These children of Abraham still believed, but it was growing difficult. Struggle and pain threatened to so dominate them that they would forget their God or despair of his concern.

When Paul quotes from this psalm in Romans 8, he does so in light of Jesus the Messiah. He employs these verses to convince his readers that *nothing shall separate us from God's love.* Paul is making the argument about discerning God's love amid unsettling circumstances: tribulation, distress, persecution, famine, nakedness, danger, and the sword (Rom 8:35). It can be easy to believe God is "for us" when things are going well in our lives. But what about during life's challenges? Here Paul draws from Psalm 44, only the meaning is now modified in light of the coming of Christ.

Originally Psalm 44 spoke of the people of Israel facing rejection and death. The question for us, and for Paul's audience, remains the same: Will God hide his face forever? Only in the life, death, and resurrection of Jesus is this question answered decisively and finally. Jesus stepped into our place to face the violence and hurt so it would not be our final or full story. Yes, we still face pain and difficulties. Paul doesn't shy away from that. But they are not the full story. They are not the sufferer's identity, which is now secure in Christ.

> No, in all these things we are more than conquerors through him who loved us. For I am sure that neither death nor life, nor angels nor rulers, nor things present nor things to come, nor powers, nor height nor depth, nor anything else in all creation, will be able to separate us from the love of God in Christ Jesus our Lord. (Rom 8:37-39)

Those who know the full story of redemption can experience joy even during suffering. Those who don't know the story are left only with despair or efforts of self-improvement.

In Jesus the Son of God, we discover God's solidarity with us, not just a fellow feeling but a *redemptive* solidarity. He absorbs our sin and enters into our pain, including our physical suffering and even death, not merely to better understand it but in order to overcome it.

In Christ we are secure. We can have confidence based not on our own faithfulness but on the faithfulness of our triune God. This God who began a good work in us will never abandon us (Phil 1:6). Nothing—not enemies, not the devil, not our pain nor nightmares—nothing shall snatch us out of his hand (Jn 10:28-29). In the power of the Spirit we are united to the Son so that we may live in the Father's grace and love.

Beloved, amid the trials and tribulations of life, let us have confidence not in ourselves, not in our own efforts, but in God. This God has come in Christ, and he has overcome sin, death, and the devil. While we may currently be walking through the shadow of death, may our God's love, grace, and compassion become ever more real to us. And may we, as the church, participate in the ongoing divine motions and movements of grace as God meets people in their need.

ACKNOWLEDGMENTS

Theology is best done in community. Period. If this book is helpful to anyone, then I have a myriad of people to thank. This is always my favorite part of writing a book, but also one of the most difficult as I try to keep it relatively brief.

Our community has been such a support to us through the last eight years. We have grown to love Covenant College, not because it is perfect but because it has become like family to us. Faculty, staff, students, and alumni have been prayerful, sensitive, and reliably encouraging. Similarly, the church has loved us well. Living in a time when organized religion is too easily belittled, New City Fellowship and Lookout Mountain Presbyterian Church have helped us echo the ancient confession "I *believe* in the holy catholic church . . ." They model how the church is not merely about a particular building but catholic (universal), seeking to be holy by elevating love and the gospel for the neighbor in need. The church may be far from perfect, but this is also where God promises to work: here beauty is found in weakness as we rest together in the love of the Father, the grace of the Son, and the fellowship of the Spirit.

Though we had been wrestling with the realities of suffering for some time, I was not planning to write a book on this subject. However, out of nowhere God provided the impetus and resources for this project to begin. Significantly, I was offered a Visiting Research Fellow position at the Center for Christian Thought at Biola University for spring 2014. While the opinions expressed in this publication are mine and do not necessarily reflect the views of the John

Templeton Foundation or CCT, this book was made possible through the support of a generous grant from the John Templeton Foundation. Thank you to all who helped my family relocate to California for those five months. That experience was rich, and my thinking was greatly helped by sharing the time with Steve Porter, Thomas Crisp, C. Stephen Evans, David Horner, William Struthers, James Wilhoit, Betsy Barber, Christopher Kaczor, John Coe, Greg Peters, James K. A. Smith, Robert Emmons, Peter Hill, Gerald Sittser, Rachel Dee, Evan Rosa, Ellen Charry, Dave Strobolakos, Oliver and Claire Crisp, Matt Jenson, Fred Sanders, Uche Anizor, and others.

I would deeply love to write a paragraph or sentence for each person explaining the distinctive way they have been instrumental in this book's formation. But space limitations make that impossible. However, I must at least say that this book simply would not be what it is without the following people: Bob Harbert, Caroline Berry, Randy Nabors, Joe Novenson, Todd Billings, John Yates, Hannah Cohen, Kevin Smith, Jim Pickett, Paige Hudson, Cal Boroughs, Render Caines, Eric Youngblood, Sarah and Mark Huffines, Lynn and Jeff Hall, Derek Halverson, Nola Stephens, Paul Morton, Elissa Weichbrodt, Brian Salter, Jared Huffman, Kyle and Shannon Taylor, Kelly and David Paschall, Scott Jones, Herb Ward, Hans Madueme, Dan Mac-Dougall, Ken Stewart, Christiana Fitzpatrick, Grant Lowe, Matt Vos, Ann Marie Granberry, Matthew O'Hearn, Christopher Green, Anna Clark, T. C. Ham, Heather and Kenny McGibbon, Katie Jo Ramsey, Randal Rauser, Jimmy Myers, who prepared the index, and Erin Fray. Thank you all for sharing your time, your stories, your wisdom, your editing skills, and your lives with me. You have offered insight, encouragement, and often-needed grace, each in your own way. Also students and auditors who took my course "Faith and Suffering," reading most of the manuscript in an earlier form, provided invaluable feedback and assistance.

Friends are like pillars that keep a house from collapsing. I would like to mention three pillars for my soul. Two of my best friends in the world, Jay Green and Jeff Morton, have been stunning gifts from God over the past sixteen years. Living in a culture that is sometimes frightened of male vulnerability, you two have modeled grace, authenticity, and personal love to me. Your ability to make me laugh and your willingness to weep, hurt, and hope with and for my family is something I treasure. And Danny Kapic, how often I have leaned on you? Thank you for your constant prayers, consistent empathy, concrete support, and your ability to make my family laugh. While I wish we lived closer, your love can be felt over the thousands of miles that separate us.

This year and next year mark the fiftieth wedding anniversaries for both my parents (Gary and Linda) and Tabitha's parents (John and Lynne). That makes one hundred years of marriage between the two couples! Thank you for giving us the inestimable gift of showing steadfastness during some very low valleys when it would have been easy for you to give up. I have no doubt but that Tabitha and I draw on your reserves in ways we don't even realize. Thank you for not only modeling faithfulness but seeking to care for us through our own challenging years. You have been a constant source of encouragement and support. As family, Jennifer and Ming, Danny and Emily, and David and Jen, you have walked this journey with us, offering support in countless ways, from plane tickets to personal notes. Thank you for making your expressions of love tangible.

I know people often talk about the need to have kids look up to their parents, but I have to say, in many ways, I look up to my children. Jonathan and Margot, you two amaze me with your compassion, patience, courage, and willingness to trust God even amid truly hard times. Pain and suffering are not hypothetical to you. By God's grace you have resisted hardening your hearts, but instead you have reminded us of God's kindness and all that we have to be thankful for. You are both unique and distinctly gifted, but your sweet friendship and faithful presence to your mother and me is like balm for our souls. Thank you for being quick to forgive us, to make us laugh, and to help us see the wonder of God's world. We love you so much.

How do I express my gratitude and love for Tabitha? You simply cannot know me well if you don't also know my wife. I don't say that simply because we have been married over twenty-three years nor to be sappy or falsely romantic. I say that because I don't think I know who I am without her. Some people might panic and write me a correction when they read my confession, encouraging me to find an identity as an individual or that I should only have my identity in Christ. But I have to say, the way God has helped me understand who I am is not as an isolated individual but as a child of God who has walked most of this pilgrimage hand in hand with Tabitha. With her brilliant mind and quick wit, her thoughtful wisdom and painful honesty, her concern for justice and her stunning willingness to push forward even amid hardships, she has in countless ways helped me understand God, his kingdom, other people, and even myself. Those who know her can honestly say Tabitha is one of the most unique, exceptionally gifted people they know. She is certainly an anchor for our family, consistently encouraging us to follow Christ in *this* world, not an imaginary one. She doesn't deny or sugarcoat the challenges, but she has helped us to see God's grace in the midst of the hardships, not just in their absence. Tabitha, as Christ embodies hope for his people, you have helped me and so many others understand that hope in personal, honest, and beautiful ways. I know of no one else in the entire world like you. Know how deeply you are loved.

NOTES

1 HARD THOUGHTS ABOUT GOD

[1]For a recent printing of the essay, see Simone Weil, "The Love of God and Affliction," in *Waiting for God*, trans. Emma Craufurd (New York: Harper Perennial Modern Classics, 2009), 67-82.

[2]I will say that sometimes in the literature of this kind, most notably in Dorothee Soelle [sometimes Sölle, see esp. her *Suffering* (Philadelphia: Fortress, 1975)], more problems are created than solved. To put it in an overly simplistic way, I fear that Soelle, and even Weil, too often reduces the challenge of faith to human activism, upholds human sympathy in a way that shortchanges eschatological hope, and substitutes the profundities of divine absence for the promises of divine presence. For more on this, including brief engagement particularly with Soelle, see Kelly M. Kapic, "Faith, Hope, and Love," in *Sanctification: Explorations in Theology and Practice*, ed. Kelly M. Kapic (Downers Grove, IL: IVP Academic, 2014), 212-31.

[3]For a brilliant explanation to nonsufferers of what this is like from the perspective of one who deals with daily pain, read Christine Miserandino's "Spoon Theory," *Butyoudontlooksick.com*, accessed July 13, 2016, www.butyoudontlooksick.com /articles/written-by-christine/the-spoon-theory. (Christine has lupus.)

[4]Stephen Crane, "A Man Said to the Universe," 1899.

[5]John Owen, *The Works of John Owen*, ed. William H. Goold (London: Banner of Truth Trust, 1965), 2:34-35; 6:570; 7:21; 11:390-91, 581.

[6]For a classic attempt to understand how people develop certain (mis)conceptions of God, see Ana-Maria Rizzutto, *The Birth of the Living God: A Psycho-Analytic Study* (Chicago: University of Chicago Press, 1981). Rizzutto draws heavily on object relations theory.

[7]Owen, *Works*, 2:34.

[8]Ibid., 35.

[9]Ibid., 11:390.

[10]Ibid.

[11]For the surprising look at the "driving force" that questions about healing and suffering play across Christian traditions, see Amanda Porterfield, *Healing in the History of Christianity* (New York: Oxford University Press, 2005).

2 DON'T ANSWER WHY

[1]It should be admitted that some find theodicies meaningful, but normally this is in order to help remove unnecessary obstacles some might have to the Christian faith. For an accessible and brief survey of various theodicies, see Richard Rice, *Suffering and the Search for Meaning: Contemporary Responses to the Problem of Pain* (Downers Grove, IL: IVP Academic, 2014).

[2]Alvin Plantinga, *God, Freedom, and Evil* (New York: Harper & Row, 1974), 63.

[3]Ibid., 63-64.

[4]See John S. Feinberg, "A Journey in Suffering: Personal Reflections on the Religious Problem of Evil," in *Suffering and the Goodness of God*, ed. Christopher W. Morgan and Robert A. Peterson (Wheaton, IL: Crossway, 2008), 213-37. Feinberg's essay pointed me back to Plantinga's treatise, which he draws from. See also Feinberg, *Where Is God? A Personal Story of Finding God in Grief and Suffering* (Nashville: Broadman, 2004). More recently philosopher Douglas Groothuis wrote similarly in his moving article "When Islands of Meaning Sink Beneath Us," in *Christianity Today* 59, no. 9 (November 2015), 50-55.

[5]John Swinton, *Raging with Compassion: Pastoral Responses to the Problem of Evil* (Grand Rapids: Eerdmans, 2007), 32-45.

[6]Alasdair MacIntyre, "Is Understanding Religion Compatible with Believing?," in *Rationality*, ed. Bryan R. Wilson (Oxford: Basil Blackwell, 1977), 62, quoted in ibid., 34. See also Kenneth Surin, *Theology and the Problem of Evil* (Eugene, OR: Wipf & Stock, 2004); and Stanley Hauerwas, *Naming the Silences: God, Medicine, and the Problem of Suffering* (Grand Rapids: Eerdmans, 1990), 39-58.

[7]Hauerwas, *Naming the Silences*, 52.

[8]The three observations come from Swinton, who then unpacks them in his own way. See his *Raging with Compassion*, 17-29.

[9]It is worth noting that philosophical axioms can actually be helpful here, as long as they are bound by the path of wisdom, displaying a moral sense and deployed with the social tact to listen, cry, and embrace. Such wise and compassionate counselors have learned not to subjugate their humanness to speculative philosophizing. But this is much harder than most of us realize.

3 LONGING AND LAMENT

[1]I should note that this is still a valid personal choice of the mourning family and is acceptable in some cultures, but we should not let cultural tradition tell us that death is okay or that suffering is not painful.

[2]There is some debate in Old Testament scholarship about the relationship between "laments" and funeral dirges, though I am sympathetic with the position that these are often blended together in various ways in Scripture, and hard and fast divides between them are not easily maintained. But such a discussion is well beyond what we can enter into here. On a different point, while the Protestant Reformation is

known for the slogan "justification by faith," in America we have come to believe in "justification by death," as if all one needs to do is die and everything is made right with God and others.

[3]For the full story see Eugene Peterson's foreword in Michael Card, *A Sacred Sorrow: Reaching Out to God in the Lost Language of Lament* (Colorado Springs: NavPress, 2005), 11-12.

[4]See Patrick Miller, "Heaven's Prisoners: The Lament as Christian Prayer," in *Lament: Reclaiming Practices in Pulpit, Pew, and Public Square*, ed. S. A. Brown and P. D. Miller (Louisville, KY: Westminster John Knox, 2005), 15-26.

[5]Daniel J. Simundson, "Suffering," in *Anchor Yale Bible Dictionary*, ed. David Noel Freedman and Gary A. Herion (New Haven, CT: Yale University Press, 1992), 6:222.

[6]For more on mourning in relation to issues of injustice and suffering, see Kelly M. Kapic and Matthew Vos, "Blessed Are Those Who Mourn," in *Cultural Encounters* 9, no. 2 (Summer 2014): 89-94.

[7]Here I use Bob's real name because many in our community at Covenant College will recognize who I am talking about and because he was willing to have his lament and story made public with the hope that it might help others. Bob has been a great gift to our community and a gracious friend to me.

[8]I am here summarizing her work, Jeanette Mathews, "Framing Lament: Providing a Context for the Expression of Pain," in *Spiritual Complaint: The Theology and Practice of Lament*, ed. M. Beier and Tim Bulkelely (Eugene, OR: Pickwick, 2013), esp. 187-89.

[9]While widely agreed upon in its basic form, for this simple structure and the following comments I'm drawing from "Lament Psalms," in *Dictionary of Biblical Imagery*, ed. Leland Ryken, James C. Wilhoit, and Tremper Longman III (Downers Grove, IL: InterVarsity Press, 1998). I have added quotes from Psalm 22, just to help the reader have concrete examples of the various elements.

[10]Kathleen O'Connor, *Lamentations and the Tears of the World* (Maryknoll: Orbis, 2002), 14, cited in Mathews, "Framing Lament," 193.

[11]Nancy L. deClaissé-Walford reviews this background and uses one particular psalm (44) as a test case: "Psalm 44: O God, Why Do You Hide Your Face?," in *My Words Are Lovely: Studies in the Rhetoric of the Psalms*, ed. Robert Foster and David Howard, London Library of Hebrew Bible/Old Testament Studies (London: T&T Clark, 2007), 121-46. Other potential communal laments could be added, such as Ps 12.

[12]For further reflections alone these lines, see Kelly M. Kapic, "Psalm 22: Forsakenness and the God Who Sings," in *Theological Commentary: Evangelical Perspectives*, ed. R. Michael Allen (London: T&T Clark, 2011), 41-56, esp. 48-51. For a fuller treatment of Jesus' laments see Rebekah Eklund, *Jesus Wept: The Significant of Jesus' Laments in the New Testament* (London: Bloomsbury, 2015).

[13]Sally A. Brown and Patrick Miller, eds., *Lament: Reclaiming Practices in Pulpit, Pew, and Public Square* (Louisville, KY: Westminster John Knox, 2005), xix.

4 EMBRACING OUR EMBODIMENT

[1]Thomas E. Reynolds, *Vulnerable Communion: A Theology of Disability and Hospitality* (Grand Rapids: Brazos, 2008).

[2]This myth is outlined by Plato in his *Phaedrus*. Similar themes are also found in his *Meno*, where Socrates explains the theory of recollection. This theory suggests that the soul exists prior to embodiment, and thus the embodied human person merely has to *recollect* in order to know the truth about the Real. For background and scholarly debate about how he understood this fall, see D. D. McGibbon, "The Fall of the Soul in Plato's Phaedrus," in *The Classical Quarterly*, n.s. 14, no. 1 (May 1964): 56-63. See also Brian Davies, *An Introduction to the Philosophy of Religion* (New York: Oxford University Press, 2004), 289-91. Davies provides a brief introduction to Plato's conception as well as the Cartesian conception that stayed within the Platonic vein.

[3]Plato actually says, "Every seeker after wisdom knows that up to the time when philosophy takes over his soul is a helpless prisoner, chained hand and foot inside the body, forced to view reality not directly but only through the prison bars, and wallowing in utter ignorance" (*Phaedo* 82d-82e, trans. G. M. A Grube [Indianapolis: Hackett, 1997]).

[4]The early church came to call this idea of creation "*ex nihilo*," arguing from the assumptions of various Scriptures and the implications of these assumptions that God's creation was not out of eternal matter (since only God is eternal), but all was at some point made by the Lord himself, who then through some amount of time brought order and design to his creation. For more on the history of this see Gerhard May, *Creatio Ex Nihilo: The Doctrine of "Creation Out of Nothing" in Early Christian Thought*, trans. A. S. Worrall (London: T&T Clark, 2004).

[5]For two classic studies on this Old Testament conception of the person, see Aubrey Johnson, *The Vitality of the Individual in the Thought of Ancient Israel*, 2nd ed. (Eugene, OR: Wipf & Stock, 2006); Hans Walter Wolff, *Anthropology of the Old Testament* (Philadelphia: Fortress, 1974). For a sampling of more recent philosophical defenses of a holistic dualism, see, e.g., C. Stephen Evans's award-winning essay, "Separable Souls: Dualism, Selfhood, and the Possibility of Life After Death," *Christian Scholar's Review* 34, no. 3 (Spring 2005): 327-40; and Richard Swinburne, *Mind, Brain, and Free Will* (Oxford: Oxford University Press, 2013).

[6]Johnson observes, "The normal Israelite view, which dominates the conception of man in the Old Testament, is that to be in sickness of body or weakness of circumstance is to experience the disintegrating power of death, and to be brought by Yahweh to the gates of Sheol; but to enjoy good health and material prosperity is to be allowed to walk with Him in fullness of life" (*Vitality of the Individual*, 108-9).

[7]I do affirm the traditional Christian consensus regarding an intermediate state, in which after death believers go immediately to be with God. Yet it is worth noting that this state is not considered the Christian hope; the resurrection of our bodies

remains the expectation (see Westminster Shorter Catechism 37). Until then, there remains some kind of incompleteness, for we are made as embodied creatures and to exist otherwise is, one might argue, unnatural, even if better than not existing at all. The definitive study demonstrating the almost universal agreement of some form of unavoidable dualism in light of this intermediate state is made by John W. Cooper, *Body, Soul and Life Everlasting: Biblical Anthropology and the Monism-Dualism Debate*, updated ed. (Grand Rapids: Eerdmans, 2000).

[8]See especially the volumes *St. Irenaeus of Lyons Against the Heresies*, Ancient Christian Writers, 3 vols., ed. Dominic J. Unger et al. (Mahwah, NJ: Paulist Press, 1992–2012).

[9]Again, see Cooper, *Body, Soul, and Life Everlasting*.

[10]Even recent Christians who argue for nonreductive physicalism aim to prove that our physicality is who we are, yet this should not be understood in a naturalistic manner. The verdict on the success of such attempts remains to be seen, but I myself believe that in the end such views are not able to escape a reductionist account. For a nonreductive physicalist constructive attempt to move forward, see Warren Brown and Brad Strawn, *The Physical Nature of the Christian Life: Neuroscience, Psychology, and the Church* (Cambridge: Cambridge University Press, 2012).

[11]Herman Bavinck, *Reformed Dogmatics: God and Creation*, ed. John Bolt, trans. John Vriend (Grand Rapids: Baker Academic, 2004), 2:559. In this way, the human creature is utterly distinct from everything else: "He unites and reconciles within himself both heaven and earth, things both invisible and visible" (ibid., 556).

[12]Even Descartes's memorable—and deeply flawed!—focus on the pineal gland was not because he thought this body "part" was the location of the soul but rather a way to understand how the soul and body interacted.

[13]Elizabeth Lewis Hall provides an excellent summary of key cultural characteristics in different ages. I am drawing heavily from her in these following paragraphs as I summarize her observations. See Elizabeth Lewis Hall, "What Are Bodies For? An Integrative Examination of Embodiment," *Christian Scholar's Review* 39, no. 2 (Winter 2010), 159-76, this discussion of modernity is found mostly in pages 161-62. See also Luke Timothy Johnson, *The Revelatory Body: Theology as Inductive Art* (Grand Rapids: Eerdmans, 2015); James K. A. Smith, *Imagining the Kingdom: How Worship Works* (Grand Rapids: Baker Academic, 2013), 29-100.

[14]For the language of "modern baroque" and a further unpacking of this perspective with all of its concerns, see Philip A. Mellor and Chris Shilling, *Re-forming the Body: Religion, Community and Modernity* (Thousand Oaks, CA: Sage, 1997).

[15]Hall, "What Are Bodies For?," 162.

[16]For a powerful critique of this problem, especially as it has had an impact on women, see Lilian Calles Barger, *Eve's Revenge: Women and a Spirituality of the Body* (Grand Rapids: Brazos, 2003).

[17]Hall, "What Are Bodies For?," 164-65. See also Barbara L. Fredrickson and Tomi-Ann Roberts, "Objectification Theory: Toward Understanding Women's Lived

Experiences and Mental Health Risks," *Psychology of Women Quarterly* 21, no. 2 (June 1997): 173-206; Jennifer Stevens Aubrey, "The Impact of Sexually Objectifying Media Exposure on Negative Body Emotions and Sexual Self-Perceptions: Investigating the Mediating Role of Body Self-Consciousness," *Mass Communication and Society* 10, no. 1 (2007), 1-23.

[18]See Kelly R. Arora, "Models of Understanding Chronic Illness: Implications for Pastoral Theology and Care," *Journal of Pastoral Theology* 19 (2009): 22-37.

[19]Dietrich Bonhoeffer, *Creation and Fall: A Theological Exposition of Genesis 1–3*, in *Dietrich Bonhoeffer Works* (Minneapolis: Fortress, 1997), 3:76.

[20]Astute author and respected farmer Wendell Berry observes, "The formula given in Genesis 2:7 is not man = body + soul; the formula there is soul = dust + breath. According to this verse, God did not make a body and put a soul into it, like a letter into an envelope. He formed man of dust; then, by breathing His breath into it, He made the dust live. The dust formed as man and made to live, did not embody a soul; it became a soul. 'Soul' here refers to the whole creature. Humanity is thus presented to us, in Adam, not as a creature of two discrete parts temporarily glued together but as a single mystery" (Wendell Berry, *Sex, Economy, Freedom & Community* [New York: Pantheon, 1993], 106). Berry's comment was first brought to my attention by Joel Shuman and Brian Volck, *Reclaiming the Body: Christians and the Faithful Use of Modern Medicine* (Grand Rapids: Brazos, 2006), 48.

[21]Bonhoeffer, *Creation and Fall*, 76.

[22]Ibid., 77.

[23]Ibid., 79.

[24]Cf. ibid., 64-65; Karl Barth, *Church Dogmatics* (Edinburgh: T&T Clark, 1958, 1960), III/1, 228-30; III/2, 220. It should be noted that more recently theologians have cautioned against some of the extreme claims and uses that were made between God's inner-trinitarian life and our social interpersonal lives. For such a word of caution, in particular about how some claims distort classic trinitarian theology, see Steve Holmes, *The Quest for the Trinity: The Doctrine of God in Scripture, History, and Modernity* (Downers Grove, IL: IVP Academic, 2012).

[25]Bonhoeffer, *Creation and Fall*, 66.

[26]Ibid., 67.

[27]Ibid., 97.

[28]Bonhoeffer has a fascinating Christological reading here, where he weaves together connections between Adam, Christ, and us. Whereas Adam was alone and anticipated "the other person" that would bring "community," Christ, as he was "alone," "loves the other person, because Christ is the way by which the human race returned to its Creator." On our own we push others away for various reasons, and we are alone. But union with Christ connects us to God and others (ibid., 96).

[29]Ibid., 98.

[30]Ibid., 99.

[31]Ibid.

[32]Ibid.

[33]Hall, "What Are Bodies For?," 167.

[34]For more on a developmental model of relationality see Jack O. Balswick, Pamela Ebstyne King, and Kevin S. Reimer, *The Reciprocating Self: Development in Theological Perspective* (Downers Grove, IL: IVP Academic, 2005).

[35]For the classic text on this matter see Norbert Elias, *The Civilizing Process* (Malden, MA: Blackwell, 2000).

[36]This source, and even some of the wording for the rest of this paragraph, is owed to sociologist Matt Vos, who first alerted me to Gergen's work. For a fuller treatment of this topic see Matt Vos, "There's No Such Thing as Alone: From Bounded-being Accounts to the Confluence of the Saints," in *Journal of Sociology and Christianity* 6, no. 2 (October 2016): 24-36.

[37]Kenneth Gergen, *Relational Being: Beyond Self and Community* (Oxford: Oxford University Press, 2009), 9.

[38]Those Gergen draws on include including Herbert Blumer, Clifford Geertz, Charles Horton Cooley, G. H. Mead, Harold Garfinkel, Erving Goffman, and Robert Bellah, among others.

[39]Dallas Willard, *The Spirit of the Disciplines: Understanding How God Changes Lives* (New York: HarperCollins, 1988), 83.

[40]Hall, "What Are Bodies For?," 175.

5 QUESTIONS THAT COME WITH PAIN

[1]David J. Melling, "Suffering and Sanctification in Christianity," in *Religion, Health and Suffering*, ed. John R. Hinnells and Roy Porter (London: Kegan Paul, 1999), 56, see 46-63; cf. Esther Cohen, "Towards a History of European Physical Sensibility: Pain in the Later Middle Ages," in *Science in Context* 8, no. 1 (1995): 47-74. Cohen makes it clear that while people did not normally seek sensations of pain for the purpose of "pleasure" (cf. modern masochism), many did believe that such experiences could be "considered useful" (ibid., 52).

[2]*New England Primer* (Boston: J. White, 1795).

[3]Cf. Patrick Wall, *Pain: The Science of Suffering* (London: Weidenfeld & Nicolson, 1999).

[4]David H. Kelsey, *Eccentric Existence: A Theological Anthropology*, 2 vols. (Louisville, KY: Westminster John Knox, 2009), 1:176-214.

[5]Some time ago Kelsey influenced my thinking and pointed me back to this literature, but this reading of Job 10 is my own.

[6]See Katherine J. Dell, *The Book of Job as Sceptical Literature* (Berlin: Walter de Gruyter, 1991), 30-38. Thanks to Scott Jones for pointing me to this source. Cf. Murray J. Haar, "Job After Auschwitz," *Interpretation* (July 1, 1999), 265-75.

[7]T. C. Ham, "The Gentle Voice of God in Job 38," *Journal of Biblical Literature* 132, no. 3 (2013): 528.

[8]Ham notes, "The very presence of the divine speech to Job implies God's concern for the man and serves to vindicate Job" (ibid., 530). For more along these lines, see, e.g., John E. Hartley, *Book of Job*, NICOT (Grand Rapids: Eerdmans, 1988), 487; Claus Westermann, *The Structure of the Book of Job: A Form-Critical Analysis*, trans. Charles A. Muenchow (Philadelphia: Fortress, 1981), 106; David Atkinson, *The Message of Job: Suffering and Grace*, BST (Downers Grove, IL: InterVarsity Press, 1991), 138-40.

[9]Ham, "Gentle Voice of God," 530, quoting Samuel L. Terrien, "The Yahweh Speeches and Job's Responses," *Review and Expositor* 68 (1971): 498.

[10]Ham, "Gentle Voice of God," 532.

[11]Ibid., 534. He is drawing form and quoting Michael V. Fox, "Job 38 and God's Rhetoric," *Semeia* 19 (1981): 59.

[12]Ham, "Gentle Voice of God," 536.

[13]Francis I. Anderson, *Job: An Introduction and Commentary*, Tyndale Old Testament Commentaries (Downers Grove, IL: InterVarsity Press, 1976), 270; quoted in ibid., 540.

[14]Ham, "Gentle Voice of God," 541.

6 ONE WITH US: INCARNATION

[1]John Swinton, *Raging with Compassion: Pastoral Responses to the Problem of Evil* (Grand Rapids: Eerdmans, 2007), 87. Here, though underdeveloped, Swinton points in the right direction: "God's taking responsibility for evil and suffering relates to the nature of the incarnation, cross, and resurrection and God's promised continuing presence in the midst of the suffering of the world" (ibid., 88). I would say here, only if we give primacy to Christology can we fully appreciate this point of God taking responsibility. Swinton alludes to but leaves the Christological points underdeveloped.

[2]Donald Fairbairn, *Life in the Trinity: An Introduction to Theology with the Help of the Church Fathers* (Downers Grove, IL: IVP Academic, 2009), 134.

[3]Ibid., 137-38.

[4]Athanasius would later write a brief biography (or hagiography) of St. Anthony. See Carolinne White, "Life of St. Antony by Athanasius," in *Early Christian Lives* (London: Penguin, 1998), 1-70.

[5]Athanasius, *On the Incarnation* (Crestwood, NY: St. Vladimir's Seminary Press, 2003), 26.

[6]John Cooper argues that such a perspective (though he does not mention Athanasius here) is similar to Old Testament views of salvation: "Their [the ancient Israelites'] hope is for a New Jerusalem and a new earth, a place where the existence of the Lord's people will again be what it was created to be in the beginning. Human life is tied to the earth. There is not 'pie in the sky by-and-by' for the individual at death, no heaven for the liberated soul" (John Cooper, *Body, Soul, and Life Everlasting* [Grand Rapids: Eerdmans, 2000], 37).

[7] Athanasius, *On the Incarnation*, 26.

[8] Ibid.

[9] Ibid., 32.

[10] Ibid. Some might take statements like this, and other language used throughout the treatise, to argue that Athanasius must be a universalist, believing all in the end will be saved. Yet, at the end of the work, he makes it clear that space for judgment remains for those who choose to remain in darkness (see e.g., p. 95).

[11] Ibid., §7.

[12] E.g., "The Word assumed a human body, expressly in order that He might offer it in sacrifice for other like bodies" (ibid., 36; cf. § 44).

[13] Ibid., 81.

[14] Augustine, *True Religion*, in *On Christian Belief*, ed. Boniface Ramsey, vol. 1/8, Works of Saint Augustine (New York: New City Press, 2005), 47 (15.29).

[15] These quotes come from ibid., 48 (16.30).

[16] Ibid., 29.

[17] Ibid., 33.

[18] Ibid., 34. "The body of the Word, then, being a real human body, in spite of its having been uniquely formed from a virgin, was of itself mortal and, like other bodies, liable to death" (ibid., 49).

[19] The classic stories of the Greeks, notes Athanasius, can speak of healings through herbal remedies and the like, but when compared with the reality of the incarnation, who "instead of just healing a wound, He both fashioned essential being and restored to health the thing that He had formed" (ibid., 87).

[20] For more on this idea, see Kelly M. Kapic, "Trajectories of a Trinitarian Eschatology," in *Trinitarian Soundings in Systematic Theology*, ed. Paul Metzger (Edinburgh: T&T Clark, 2005), 189-202.

[21] See, e.g., Athanasius, *On the Incarnation*, §11-12, §32.

[22] Consider Athanasius's famous line that the Son "assumed humanity that we might become God": to understand his comment we need to read the statement within its immediate context. He is reflecting on the marvelous scandal of the Son's condescension, and that as the Word becomes flesh, he makes known to us the reality of the Father. The next sentence is clear: "He manifested Himself by means of a body in order that we might perceive the Mind of the unseen Father" (*On the Incarnation*, 93). In this section Athanasius seems to point to both ontic and noetic directions as he unpacks the "Saviour's achievements." I am highlighting here the noetic ones, but to be fair to this early father, he is also making significant ontic claims about the life of God in us, but this is more than can be unpacked here. The point is that with the Son's humiliation, part of how we become "like God" is *because* we see the Father through the Son. We do not become mini-omniscient gods, but rather we see the Father through the eyes of the incarnate Son, and in this way we become like the Son.

[23]Ibid., 38.

[24]B. B Warfield, "The Emotional Life of Our Lord," in *The Person and Work of Christ* (Philadelphia: Presbyterian & Reformed, 1950), esp. 93-145.

[25]See, for example, the language of the Nicene-Constantinople Creed, which affirms that the "one Lord Jesus Christ, the Son of God," is "True God of True God; begotten, not made," but also, in light of our need of salvation, "became man . . . suffered, died, and was buried." And see also the more developed language and distinctions employed in the Chalcedonian Definition.

[26]For more on Warfield's life, see David B. Calhoun, *Princeton Seminary,* vol. 2, *The Majestic Testimony 1869-1929* (Edinburgh: Banner of Truth, 1996), esp. 118, 311-27; Hugh T. Kerr, "Warfield: The Person Behind the Theology," lecture presented at Princeton Theological Seminary, Spring 1982.

[27]Cf. Paul Helm's essay that warns against too closely trying to equate Jesus' emotions with God's without careful distinction. See Paul Helm, "B. B. Warfield on Divine Passion," *Westminster Theological Journal* 69 (2007): 94-104.

[28]The fullest studies to date on this theme are in the recent work by Stephen Voorwinde. He provides an extensive treatment of John's Gospel in *Jesus' Emotions in the Fourth Gospel: Human or Divine?* (London: T&T Clark, 2005), and a fuller overview of all four Gospels one at a time in his *Jesus' Emotions in the Gospels* (London: T&T Clark, 2011).

[29]Warfield, "Emotional Life," 96.

[30]Ibid., 100.

[31]Ibid., 115.

[32]Ibid., 116-17.

[33]Athanasius, *On the Incarnation*, §6.

7 ONE FOR US: CROSS

[1]For more on this tension between medieval Roman Catholic and then early Protestant conceptions of the Passion, followed by modern Catholic Counter Reformation reactions, see Jan Frans van Dijkhuizen, "Partakers of Pain: Religious Meanings of Pain in Early Modern England," in *The Sense of Suffering: Constructions of Physical Pain in Early Modern Culture,* ed. Jan Frans van Dijkhuizen and Karl A. E. Enenkel (Leiden: Brill, 2009), 189-220.

[2]Athanasius, *On the Incarnation* (New York: St. Vladimir's Seminary Press, 2003), 51; emphasis added.

[3]Chrysostom argued that "his taking flesh to suffer what he suffered is a far greater thing than creating the world out of things that are not. This is indeed a token of his loving-kindness, but the other far more." Erik M. Heen and Philip D. W. Krey, eds., *Hebrews,* Ancient Christian Commentary on Scripture 10 (Downers Grove, IL: InterVarsity Press, 2005), 43; ICCS/Accordance electronic ed.

[4]Here I slightly modify the end of this verse in ESV to include sisters, which the ESV

itself recognizes as legitimate in their notes. The point of the text is identification with humanity, not one particular sex.

[5]"We are united to the Son of God by a bond so close, that we can find in our nature that holiness of which we are in want; for he not only as God sanctifies us, but there is also the power of sanctifying in his human nature, not that it has it from itself, but that God had poured upon it a perfect fullness of holiness, so that from it we may all draw." John Calvin, *Calvin's Commentaries (Complete),* trans. John King (Edinburgh: Calvin Translation Society, 1847), n.p.; Accordance electronic ed.

[6]Karl Barth, *Church Dogmatics* (Edinburgh: T&T Clark, 1961), IV/1, 176.

[7]See Bertrand Russell, "Knowledge by Acquaintance and Knowledge by Description," *Proceedings of the Aristotelian Society* 11 (1910–1911): 108-28; cf. "On the Nature of Acquaintance," *Monist* 24 (1914): 161-87. Similarly, it might be worth considering if in the incarnation the Son gains what Michael Polanyi describes as "personal knowledge."

[8]Tucked in near the end of the beautiful but complex book of Isaiah, we discover a series of what are called "servant songs" (Is 42:1-9; 49:1-13; 50:4-11; 52:13–53:12 [cf. Is 51:13; 61:1-11]). In these texts a strange servant figure emerges who represents and sacrificially serves others. Consistently associated with corporate Israel (cf. Is 41:8-10), this servant can also point to an individual who is meant to represent the whole (cf. Is 11:1-5; 32:1-8). Remnant theology—in which a part could represent a whole—is assumed here: the king was expected to represent Israel, and Israel was intended to be a blessing to the nations (cf. Gen 12:1-3). The expectation is of a time of renewal brought about by God's "servant" (Is 42:1). Jesus draws heavily from these songs as he frames and communicates his own identity, though most will not at first recognize all the connections he was making.

[9]See Ludwig Koehler and Walter Baumgartner, *The Hebrew and Aramaic Lexicon of the Old Testament* (New York: E. J. Brill, 1994), 318. Cf. Klaus Baltzer, *Deutero-Isaiah: A Commentary on Isaiah 40–55,* trans. Margaret Kohl, ed. Peter Machinist (Minneapolis: Fortress, 2001), 406-7. This is not new, as for example the Luther Bible translated it as "Krankheit," which means "illness" or "sickness." Cf. Jeremy Schipper, *Disability and Isaiah's Suffering Servant* (Oxford: Oxford University Press, 2011); he argues that the forms of *hlh* in Isaiah 53 are employed in reference to the servant's condition, suggesting "a disability more than a physical injury afflicted by humans" (ibid., 44).

[10]Basil the Great, quoted in Michal Jinkins and Stephen Breck Reid, "God's Forsakenness: The Cry of Dereliction as an Utterance Within the Trinity," *Horizons in Biblical Theology* 19, no 1 (June 1, 1997): 45.

[11]For background studies on Isaiah 53 and especially on how it's understood in the New Testament, see Darrell Bock and Mitch Glaser, *The Gospel According to Isaiah 53: Encountering the Suffering Servant in Jewish and Christian Theology* (Grand

Rapids: Kregel, 2012); Peter Stuhlmacher and Bernd Janowski, eds., *The Suffering Servant: Isaiah 53 in Jewish and Christian Sources*, trans. Daniel P. Bailey (Grand Rapids: Eerdmans, 2004).

[12]Because the word *man* is able to convey both the individual and the universal at the same time, this term has an important theological significance far beyond debates about gender and language. It is for this reason that I think this term, in these particular kinds of cases, is worth preserving.

[13]Paul L. Gavrilyuk, "God's Impassible Suffering in the Flesh: The Promise of Paradoxical Christology," in *Divine Impassibility and the Mystery of Human Suffering*, ed. James F. Keating and Thomas Joseph White (Grand Rapids: Eerdmans, 2009), 143. For a fuller historical treatment see Paul L. Gavrilyuk, *The Suffering of the Impassable God: The Dialectics of Patristic Thought*, Oxford Early Christian Studies (Oxford: Oxford University Press, 2004).

[14]Cf. Gavrilyuk, "God's Impassible Suffering in the Flesh," 145.

8 RISEN AND REMAINING

[1]Here and the following paragraphs I freely move between paraphrasing and quoting from Friedrich Nietzsche, *The Gay Science*, trans. Walter Kaufmann (New York: Vintage, 1974), 181-82. All direct quotes come from these two pages, unless otherwise noted.

[2]Cf. Friedrich Wilhelm Nietzsche, *Beyond Good and Evil: Prelude to a Philosophy of the Future* (New York: Vintage, 1989).

[3]Cf. Friedrich Nietzsche, *The Will to Power*, ed. Walter Kaufmann (New York: Vintage, 1968).

[4]Not only rich, this Jewish leader was considered a "good and righteous man" (Mt 27:57; Lk 23:50) and a "respected member of the council" (Mk 15:43). Along the way, Joseph had also apparently become a disciple of Jesus (Jn 19:38).

[5]While many Bibles still include Mark 16:9-20, it is widely accepted that this is a later addition to the biblical text and not part of the original. For more on this, see R. T. France, *The Gospel of Mark*, in New International Greek Testament Commentary (Grand Rapids: Eerdmans, 2002), 685-88; Bruce M. Metzger, *Textual Commentary on the Greek New Testament*, 2nd ed. (New York: United Bible Societies, 1994), 101-7. For a roundtable discussion on this debate, see David Alan Black, ed., *Perspectives on the Ending of Mark: Four Views* (Nashville: Broadman & Holman, 2008).

[6]For more on how Jesus was incorporated within the divine identity by the early church as they sought to respond faithfully to the fuller self-revelation of God, see Richard Bauckham, *Jesus and the God of Israel* (Grand Rapids: Eerdmans, 2008).

[7]Cf. 1 John: this Jesus they "heard" and had "seen" with their own eyes, they "looked upon" him and even "touched him with our hands" (1 Jn 1:1). This Jesus, who lived, died, and then rose from the dead, was the personification of the Word of life: "the life was made manifest, and we have seen it, and testify to it and proclaim to you

the eternal life . . . which we have seen and heard" (1 Jn 1:2-3). To encounter this risen Jesus was to be drawn into fellowship with the children of God and with God himself (cf. 1 Jn 1:3).

[8]They would one day die again, and thus a distinction might be made between temporary *resuscitation* from the dead (e.g., Lazarus) and eternal life secured by *resurrection* from the dead (Jesus).

[9]Cf. N. T. Wright, *The Resurrection of the Son of God*, Christian Origins and the Question of God 3 (Minneapolis: Fortress, 2003), 719-38.

[10]See the classic examples of this way of thinking modeled by Rudolf Bultmann (1884–1976) and the more recent advocate John Dominic Crossan (1934–). For a helpful review of various approaches that deny a bodily resurrection, see David Ferguson, "Interpreting the Resurrection," *Scottish Journal of Theology* 38 (1985): 287-305.

[11]For a devastating critique of the consequences of an approach that denies a bodily resurrection as modeled in so many modern theologians, see Paul D. Molnar, *Incarnation and Resurrection: Toward a Contemporary Understanding* (Grand Rapids: Eerdmans, 2007). Sadly, this is not a small mistake; it is massive. As Molnar has shown in great detail, failing to affirm a literal bodily resurrection of Jesus affects not simply what you say about a tomb but about the person of Jesus and ultimately about the triune God and salvation. I would add, denying Jesus' resurrection renders pastoral ministry vacuous to those who suffer physically.

[12]Cf., e.g., Larry W. Hurtado, who employs this observation to differentiate early Christian affirmations from later writings (e.g., Gospel of Thomas) in his masterful *Lord Jesus Christ: Devotion to Jesus in Earliest Christianity* (Grand Rapids: Eerdmans, 2003), 476.

[13]George Eldon Ladd, *I Believe in the Resurrection of Jesus* (Grand Rapids: Eerdmans, 1975), 34. Throughout Ladd's book he makes clear that for the apostles, a genuine physical resurrection was central to their understanding and message.

[14]*Catholic* here means "universal," as Christ's bodily resurrection was affirmed by Eastern Orthodoxy, Roman Catholicism, and all the main historic Protestant traditions.

[15]For more on this see the brilliant work by Richard B. Hays, *Reading Backwards: Figural Christology and the Fourfold Gospel Witness* (Waco, TX: Baylor University Press, 2014). Cf. Christopher J. H. Wright, *Knowing Jesus Through the Old Testament*, 2nd ed. (Downers Grove, IL: IVP Academic, 2014).

[16]Wright, *Resurrection of the Son of God*, 661.

[17]For a classic orthodox unpacking of questions related to the continuing humanity of Jesus (with a real human body) in terms of his resurrection, ascension, and ongoing heavenly session, see Thomas Aquinas, *Summa Theologica* 4.3.Q54-59, trans. Fathers of the English Dominican Province (1947; repr., Allen, TX: Christian Classics, 1981), 2307-36.

[18]Didymus of Alexandria, *Commentary on the Psalms* 259, quoted in *1 Corinthians Interpreted by Early Christian Commentators*, trans. and ed. Judith L. Kovacs (Grand Rapids: Eerdmans, 2005), 271.

[19]This is why theologians and biblical scholars sometimes speak of the gift of the "Christ event," which is shorthand for the incarnation, death, resurrection, and ascension of Jesus.

[20]John Owen, *The Works of John Owen*, ed. William H. Goold (London: Banner of Truth Trust, 1965), 1:247.

[21]Ibid., 1:238-39.

[22]Hilary of Poitiers, *On the Trinity* 11.16, in Nicene and Post-Nicene Fathers, 2nd Series (1899; repr., Peabody, MA: Hendrickson, 1994), 9:207.

[23]See, e.g., Kelly M. Kapic and Wesley Vander Lugt, "The Ascension of Jesus and the Descent of the Holy Spirit in Patristic Perspective: A Theological Reading," *Evangelical Quarterly* 79, no. 1 (2007), 23-32; Gerrit Scott Dawson, *Jesus Ascended: The Meaning of Christ's Continuing Incarnation* (London: T&T Clark, 2004).

[24]*Where* and *how* this can be is open to debate, but that he does not abandon his body is certainly part of classic orthodoxy. For recent attempts to make sense of the "where" question, for example, see T. F. Torrance, *Space, Time, and Resurrection* (Grand Rapids, Eerdmans, 1976); and Douglas Farrow, *Ascension and Ecclesia* (Grand Rapids: Eerdmans, 1999).

[25]For an excellent theological and pastoral unpacking of this, see Dawson's *Jesus Ascended*. It is true that Lutheran and Reformed debates about the Lord's Supper often break out at this point, since questions about the ascended Christ being "in," "with," and "under" the elements strikes many as compromising the continuing humanity of Jesus. But to engage this debate here is more than we can do.

[26]Owen, *Works*, 1:239. He adds, "We believe that the very same body wherein he suffered for us, without any alteration as unto its substance, essence, or integral parts, and not another body, of an ethereal, heavenly structure, wherein is nothing of flesh, blood, or bones, by which he so frequently testified the faithfulness of God in his incarnation, is still that temple wherein God dwells, and wherein he administers in the holy place not made with hands."

[27]Augustine, *True Religion*, in *On Christian Belief*, ed. Boniface Ramsey, 1/8 in Works of Saint Augustine (New York: New City Press, 2005), 49 (16.32).

9 FAITH, HOPE, AND LOVE

[1]This chapter, though revised at points, draws heavily from an essay I published earlier. This essay was the impetus for not just this chapter but this book as a whole. For the original, see "Faith, Hope, and Love: A Theological Meditation on Suffering and Sanctification," in *Sanctification: Explorations in Theology and Practice*, ed. Kelly M. Kapic (Downers Grove, IL: InterVarsity Press, 2014), 212-31.

[2]Søren Kierkegaard, *Fear and Trembling; Repetition,* ed. Howard Vincent Hong and Edna Hatlestad Hong (Princeton, NJ: Princeton University Press, 1983), 121-22.

[3]Ibid., 122.

[4]Ibid., 123.

[5]*Fear and Trembling* comes right out of the "Pauline and Lutheran tradition to which Kierkegaard belonged" (Ronald M. Green, "'Developing' *Fear and Trembling,*" in *The Cambridge Companion to Kierkegaard,* ed. Alastair Hannay and Gordon D. Marino [Cambridge: Cambridge University Press, 1998], 278). For more on Kierkegaard and Luther see, e.g., Craig Hinkson, "Luther and Kierkegaard: Theologians of the Cross," *International Journal of Systematic Theology* 3, no. 1 (2001): 27-45. Kierkegaard tended to push the demands of this faith on the individual, often because of his personality and context, while Luther was surprisingly aware of his need for others to sustain his faith, especially during seasons of weakness and suffering.

[6]Oswald Bayer noted that for Luther "justification by faith alone meant that everything was said and done; living by faith is already the new life. When, nevertheless, Luther speaks about 'sanctification' he simply talks about justification. Justification and sanctification are not for him two separate acts that we can distinguish, as though sanctification follows after justification, and has to do so. In talking about sanctification Luther stresses the institutional side of the event of justification" (*Living by Faith: Justification and Sanctification* [Grand Rapids: Eerdmans, 2003], 59).

[7]In a survey of the two-volume collection of *Luther's Correspondence and Other Contemporary Letters,* ed. and trans. Preserved Smith and Charles M. Jacobs (Philadelphia: Lutheran Publication Society, 1918), it appears that with age and experience Luther's sensitivity to the plight of physical pain becomes more pronounced—he and those he knows face such trials, and dealing with the plague furthers these reflections. Unless otherwise noted, all quotations from his letters come from this edition.

[8]In a biography of Luther's wife it is said that possibly her "biggest challenge was as a nurse, doctor, and counselor to her husband," who "suffered from many illnesses and seemed to recklessly disregard symptoms" on many occasions. "He had serious bouts of depression, attacks of dizziness, constipation, pyosis in his leg, and kidney stones" (Rudolf K. Markwald and Marilynn Morris Markwald, *Katharina von Bora: A Reformation Life* [St. Louis: Concordia, 2002], 124).

[9]E.g., *Luther's Correspondence,* letters 765, 766, p. 403-7. For more on his dealing with death as faced by others and himself, see Neil R. Leroux, *Martin Luther as Comforter: Writings on Death* (Leiden: Brill, 2007).

[10]See, e.g., how he often relied on his "pastor" for care and comfort, especially during times of illness: Martin J. Lohrmann, "Bugenhagen's Pastoral Care of Martin Luther," *Lutheran Quarterly* 24, no. 2 (2010): 125-36.

[11]*Luther's Correspondence,* letter 768, p. 409. Elsewhere he writes, "Blessed be my Christ, even amid despair, death and blasphemy!" (ibid., 786, p. 428).

[12]For a fascinating response in which he outlines who should remain and who might leave during an outbreak of the plague, see Martin Luther, "Whether One May Flee From a Deadly Plague," in *Luther's Works*, ed. Jaroslav Jan Pelikan and Helmut T. Lehmann, American ed. (St. Louis: Concordia, 1968), 43:119-38.

[13]*Luther's Correspondence*, letter 779, p. 420. He appears to be referencing Luke 22:32.

[14]David C. Steinmetz, *Luther in Context* (Grand Rapids: Baker, 1995), 31.

[15]Heiko Augustinus Oberman, *Luther: Man Between God and the Devil* (New Haven, CT: Yale University Press, 1989).

[16]At one point Luther seems to conclude that wrestling through suffering, persecution, and the endurance of evil really was the "Christian life," and to be free from them seems to entail being on the far side of glory (*Luther's Correspondence*, letter 217, p. 275).

[17]Ibid., 768, p. 409, fn. 3. Cf. Letter 779, p. 420, where he tells Nicholas Hausmann of his continued trial, which appears to be a reference to his abiding illness.

[18]Ibid., 765, p. 404. Luther does not seem here to directly link the spiritual trial with the later physical struggle, but in many ways the narrative begs for such connections.

[19]Ibid., 406. Justus Jonas wrote to Bugenhagen, the city church pastor, a letter the day after Luther's episode, recording what he said and heard because he did not want Luther's words, which were spoken "in his pain to be lost to us, for they were full of the most ardent feeling" (ibid., 764, pp. 403-4).

[20]Ibid., 765, p. 407.

[21]Ibid., 786, p. 428.

[22]Ibid., 768, p. 409.

[23]Oberman observes Luther's dependence on the prayers of others, especially for his health; so strong was this dependence that when he fell ill he wouldn't hesitate to blame others for apparently failing to pray for him (Oberman, *Luther*, 311).

[24]Søren Kierkegaard, *The Prayers of Kierkegaard* (Chicago: University of Chicago Press, 1956), 40.

[25]John Calvin, *Institutes of the Christian Religion*, Library of Christian Classics (Philadelphia: Westminster, 1960), 1:3.2.7.

[26]See Claus Westermann, *Praise and Lament in the Psalms* (Atlanta, GA: John Knox, 1981). Cf. Walter Brueggemann, *The Psalms and the Life of Faith* (Minneapolis: Fortress, 1995).

[27]Dorothee Soelle, *Suffering* (Philadelphia: Fortress, 1975), 1-32.

[28]Martin Luther, "Preface to the Psalms," in *Martin Luther: Selections from His Writings*, ed. John Dillenberger (New York: Doubleday, 1962), 39.

[29]Ibid., 40.

[30]Ibid., 40-41

[31]Oberman, *Luther*, 311.

[32]William L. Lane, *Hebrews 1-8*, ed. Ralph P. Martin, Word Biblical Commentary 47a (Dallas: Word, 1991), liii-lxii.

³³William L. Lane, *Hebrews 9-13*, ed. Ralph P. Martin, Word Biblical Commentary, 47b (Dallas: Word, 1991), 288. Here Lane is drawing from numerous folks, but quoting a bit from O. Michel, "Zur Aauslegung des Hebräerbriefes," *Novum Testamentum* 6 (1963): 189-91, 347.

³⁴Nicholas Wolterstorff, *Lament for a Son* (Grand Rapids: Eerdmans, 1987), 89.

³⁵Erich W. Gritsch, "Introduction to Church and Ministry," in Martin Luther, *Church and Ministry 1*, Luther's Works 39, ed. J. J. Pelikan, H. C. Oswald, and H. T. Lehmann (Philadelphia: Fortress, 1999), xiv.

³⁶Martin Luther, quoted by Jane E. Strohl, "Luther's Fourteen Consolations," in *The Pastoral Luther: Essays on Martin Luther's Practical Theology*, ed. Timothy J. Wengert (Grand Rapids: Eerdmans, 2009), 320, see 310-324. Cf. Robert A. Kelly, "The Suffering Church: A Study of Luther's *theologia crucis*," *Concordia Theological Quarterly* 50, no. 1 (1986): 3-17.

10 CONFESSION AND THE OTHER

¹D. A. Fishbain, "The Association of Chronic Pain and Suicide," in *Seminars in Clinical Neuropsychiatry* 3, no. 4 (July 1999): 221-27.

²We may be more than our bodies, but we are not less than them. See chapter four on embodiment for more reflections on this.

³For a full history of the etymology of "pain," see *The Oxford English Dictionary*, ed. J. A. Simpson and E. S. C. Weiner, 2nd ed. (Oxford: Clarendon, 1989), 11:66-68.

⁴See especially chapters 1-3 in this book for more on my cautions for walking down this path.

⁵D. Martyn Lloyd-Jones, *Spiritual Depression: Its Causes and Its Cure* (Grand Rapids: Eerdmans, 1965), 20.

⁶Ibid., 21.

⁷Cf. Scot McKnight, *The Letter of James*, in New International Commentary on the New Testament (Grand Rapids: Eerdmans, 2011), 445-48; Everett Ferguson, *Early Christians Speak* (Abilene, TX: Abilene Christian University Press, 1987), 181-91.

⁸Cf. Thomas N. Tentler, *Sin and Confession on the Eve of the Reformation* (Princeton, NJ: Princeton University Press, 1977).

⁹All quotations here are from the authoritative edition: Dietrich Bonhoeffer, *Life Together*, trans. Daniel W. Bloesch and ed. Geffrey B. Kelly, in Dietrich Bonhoeffer Works 5 (Minneapolis: Fortress, 1996), 1-140.

¹⁰Ibid., 112-13.

¹¹Ibid., 113.

¹²Ibid.

¹³Heidelberg Catechism, Q&A 21.

¹⁴Bonhoeffer, *Life Together*, 108.

¹⁵Ibid., 111.

¹⁶Ibid., 115. Do note that Christian psychologists, at their best, rightly avoid this criticism. For example, see Mark R. McMinn, *Why Sin Matters: The Surprising*

Relationship Between Our Sin and God's Grace (Wheaton, IL: Tyndale House, 2004); and his *Sin and Grace in Christian Counseling: An Integrative Paradigm* (Downers Grove, IL: IVP Academic, 2008).

[17]Bonhoeffer, *Life Together*, 115. I would add some warnings about younger people (e.g., high school and college students) simply confessing to one another. Young peers can provide real grace to one another, but older and more experienced believers are often needed for fuller wisdom and benefits to be realized in these often complex situations. Depending on the gravity of the confession, young people often do not have the background and ability to put what they are hearing in context, and thus it can end up hurting the one confessing or the one receiving it rather than helping.

[18]Ibid., 111.

[19]To understand this line of argument more fully, see Kelly M. Kapic, *A Little Book for New Theologians* (Downers Grove, IL: IVP Academic, 2012), 80-92.

[20]Bonhoeffer, *Life Together*, 113.

[21]Martin Luther, "The Babylonian Captivity of the Church," in *Word and Sacrament* 2, ed. Abdel Ross Wentz, Works of Martin Luther 36 (Charlottesville, VA: Fortress, 1959), 120.

[22]David B. Gowler, *James Through the Centuries* (West Sussex, UK: Wiley Blackwell, 2014), 304.

11 FAITHFUL

[1]Alison Lurie, *The Last Resort: A Novel* (New York: Henry Holt, 1998), 156-57.

[2]Eugene H. Peterson, *A Long Obedience in the Same Direction: Discipleship in an Instant Society* (Downers Grove, IL: InterVarsity Press, 2000).

[3]Paul R. House starts such a list by naming "Joseph, Joshua, Hannah, David, Jeremiah, Ezekiel, many psalmists and Job . . . joined later by Esther, Daniel and others." Paul R. House, *Old Testament Theology* (Downers Grove, IL: IVP Academic, 1998), 457-58. House's discussion of Ruth helped inform this paragraph.

[4]For a stimulating reflection on this rich book, see Carolyn Custis James, *The Gospel of Ruth: Loving God Enough to Break the Rules* (Grand Rapids: Zondervan, 2009).

[5]Stacey Floyd-Thomas et al., *Black Church Studies: An Introduction* (Nashville: Abingdon, 2007), 184.

[6]Henri Nouwen and Walter J. Ganney, *Aging: The Fulfillment of Life* (New York, Doubleday, 1976), 103.

[7]Richard H. Smith, *The Joy of Pain: Schadenfreude and the Dark Side of Human Nature* (Oxford: Oxford University Press, 2013).

[8]Dietrich Bonhoeffer, *Ethics*, in Dietrich Bonhoeffer Works 6 (Minneapolis: Fortress, 2005).

[9]For an entry-level summary of Bonhoeffer's view on this, see Lawrence's helpful *Bonhoeffer: A Guide for the Perplexed* (London: T&T Clark, 2010), 29-32.

[10] Alan Jacobs, *The Narnian* (New York: HarperCollins, 2005), 284. It is worth noting that there are legitimate concerns about some aspects of Williams's theology and his application of co-inherence. See, e.g., Barbara Newman, "Charles Williams and the Companions of the Co-inherence," *Spiritus: A Journal of Christian Spirituality* 9, no. 1 (Spring 2009): 1-26.

[11] See Walter Hooper, *C. S. Lewis: A Complete Guide to His Life & Works* (San Francisco: Harper Collins, 1996), 85-86.

[12] Dionysius, bishop of Alexandria, believed some kind of vicarious suffering even unto death happened as Christians cared for those in need: "For [Christians] were infected by others with the disease, drawing on themselves the sickness of their neighbors and cheerfully accepting their pains. Many, in nursing and curing others, transferred their death to themselves and died in their stead, turning the common formula that is normally an empty courtesy into a reality." Dionysius, quoted in Gerald L. Sittser, *Water from a Deep Well: Christian Spirituality from Early Martyrs to Modern Missionaries* (Downers Grove, IL: InterVarsity Press, 2007), 64. Whether this was simply how the plague was spread or not, Dionysius seems at times to see this as an example of what Williams would consider a "way of exchange."

[13] Phil Ryken, "Nobody Knows the Trouble I've Seen," Wheaton College, August 27, 2014, www.youtube.com/watch?v=_yVQ8xVp7kA.

[14] C. S. Lewis, *The Four Loves* (Glasgow: Fount, 1977), 111.

[15] Susan Silk and Barry Goldman, "How Not to Say the Wrong Thing," *Los Angeles Times*, April 7, 2013.

GENERAL INDEX

SCRIPTURE INDEX

A free study guide for *Embodied Hope* is available online at

ivpress.com/embodied-hope

Finding the Textbook You Need

The IVP Academic Textbook Selector
is an online tool for instantly finding the IVP books
suitable for over 250 courses across 24 disciplines.

ivpacademic.com